Grand Diplôme Cooking Course

Volume 20

Grand Diplôme Cooking Course

A Danbury Press Book

The Danbury Press

a division of Grolier Enterprises, Inc.

Robert B. Clarke Publisher

This book has been adapted from the Grand Diplôme Cooking Course, originally published by Purnell Cookery, U.S.A.

Library of Congress Catalog Card Number: 72-13896

Filmsetting by Petty and Sons Ltd., Leeds, England.
Printed in the United States of America

All recipes have been tested either at the Cordon Bleu Cookery School in London or in our U.S. test kitchens.
Note: all recipe quantities in this book serve 4 people unless otherwise stated.

Contents

MENUS

FEATURES

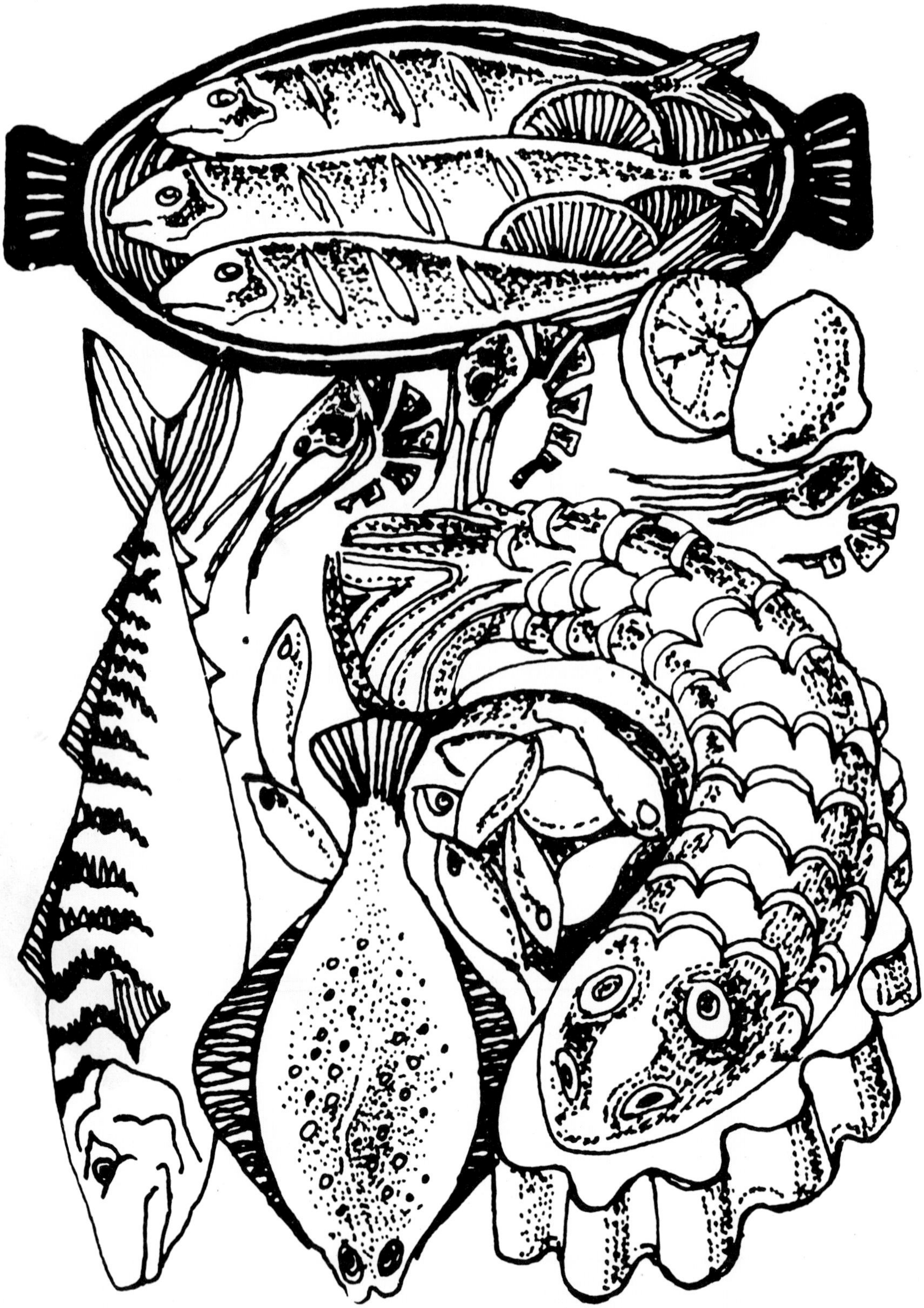

From the Editor

Simple chicken, steak and fish dishes are among our dependable stand-bys in **Quick Dishes for the Busy Cook.** In addition, we introduce you to cheese crumb flans, filled with egg, tomato, pimiento and ham mixtures.

The elegant menu from **Cooking in a Studio Apartment** is charming in its simplicity, and you'll discover many **New Ways with Vegetables** – from Stilton-baked leeks to a gratin of mushrooms with sour cream. The **Picnic for One** takes you off on an excursion by yourself, ready to enjoy a private lunch of chicken and mushroom pie, or crabmeat salad, with a slice of orange and almond gingerbread for dessert. Or you can plan to include five guests and make it an **Elegant Picnic for Six,** with individual mushroom quiches, a cold fruit and chicken curry and a choice of two desserts.

The **Barbecue for Ten** completes the menus for **Eating Out of Doors.** It includes kebabs, of course, with baked potatoes and a luscious apricot cheesecake. We have added a strawberry and orange cheesecake as a mouthwatering alternative and our suggestions for **Drinks** will help along the party spirit. If Sunday morning company is more your style, **Brunch for Ten** will give you ideas to fill up a whole, lazy day.

Volume 20 continues with **Fruit Puddings and Desserts** – a variety of interesting dishes using plums, peaches, lemons, prunes and apricots among other favorites. And in **Cooking on a Budget** we stretch your food dollar with suggestions for leftovers, and for cooking large batches of meat sauce, quiches and pizzas – all of which can be frozen.

The **Planned Party Menus** will delight those invited to your Theater Supper for Six, Buffet for Twelve, Reception for Twenty-four or – to finish on a grand note – a Party for Fifty, with canapés and cold finger food to impress the most discriminating guests. Bon Appétit!

Sheryl Julian. Joy Langridge

The finished appetizer for our first dinner party menu – poached fillets of white fish cooked in hard cider or wine, covered with sliced vegetables and coated with a creamy sauce. The entrée, a rich steak and kidney tourtière, is also shown

A DINNER MENU FROM YOUR FREEZER

Filets de Poisson Durand

Tourtière de Boeuf
Beet, Potato and Apple Salad

Coupes d'Ananas
with Petits Fours

White wine – French hard cider
or Saumur (Loire)

Red wine – Côte Rôtie (Rhône)
or Zinfandel (California)

The first course for this dinner – which you prepare with the help of your freezer – is poached fillets of flounder covered with chopped tomatoes and carrots and coated with a cream sauce. A steak, kidney and mushroom pie accompanied by a beef, potato and apple salad makes the main course. And a smooth, refreshing pineapple coupe, with a choice of two petits fours, gives you a pleasing end to this menu. The timetable on page 10 will help you through the planning and preparation.

We suggest you serve a hard cider or a dry Saumur with the fish course and change to a full-bodied red Rhône wine – a Côte Rôtie, for example – or a Zinfandel from California – to drink with the Tourtière de boeuf.

TIMETABLE

Day before
Make petits fours and store in an airtight container. Remove tourtière de boeuf from freezer and leave in refrigerator to thaw. Remove fish from freezer. Make vinaigrette dressing for salad.
Make pineapple coupe and store in freezer.

Day of party (afternoon)
Take pineapple slices from freezer and store in refrigerator. Make beet and potato salad, dress and refrigerate. Prepare chicory salad ingredients but do not dress. Prepare tomatoes for fish.

Order of Work

7:00
Set oven at 350°F. Arrange petits fours on serving dish; chill coupe glasses.

7:20
Place tourtière in heated oven. Spoon chopped tomatoes over fish.

7:40
Reheat fish below tourtière. Put pineapple parfait in refrigerator. Make sauce for fish.

8:00
Spoon sauce over fish; serve at once. Between courses: toss chicory salad and spoon pineapple parfait mixture into chilled glasses.

Cooking times in individual recipes have sometimes been adjusted to help you when cooking and serving this menu as a three-course meal.

Filets de Poisson Durand

6 large flounder fillets
1¼ cups hard cider or ¾ cup apple cider mixed with ½ cup white wine
juice of ½ lemon
¾ cup water
salt and white pepper
1 small turnip
4 carrots, thinly sliced
2 onions, thinly sliced
1 tablespoon butter
bouquet garni

To finish
3 tomatoes
3 tablespoons butter
3 tablespoons flour
¾ cup light cream
1 tablespoon chopped parsley

Method
Set the oven at 350°F. Butter an ovenproof dish and a large piece of foil to cover it.

Tuck the ends of the fillets in so they will fit into the baking dish, making sure the skinned side is underneath. Pour in half the hard cider or half the cider and wine mixture, the lemon juice, water, salt and pepper and cover with the buttered foil. Poach the fish in the preheated oven for 8 minutes.

Peel the turnip and cut it into quarters. Pare away the sharp edges and slice the turnip into thin rounds. Put the turnip with the sliced carrots and onions into a saucepan with the butter. Cook gently until the butter melts, add salt and pepper to taste and pour in the remaining hard cider (or cider and wine). Add the bouquet garni and bring to a boil. Simmer gently until the vegetables are tender and have absorbed the liquid, but take care that they do not brown.

Take the fish from the oven and very carefully tip the liquid from the dish into a container. Spread the vegetables over the fish.

To freeze Leave both the liquid and fish to cool completely, then cover the containers with their lids and cover the fish with a double thickness of foil. Freeze.

Thawing and serving Let both liquid and fish thaw in the refrigerator for 24 hours. Preheat the oven to 350°F. Scald, skin and halve the tomatoes and squeeze out the seeds. Coarsely chop them and scatter them over the other vegetables. Reheat the fish, covered with foil, in the preheated oven for 15 minutes or until fish and vegetables are both hot.

Meanwhile, melt the butter in a saucepan and stir in the flour. Cook for 2 minutes, then blend in the liquid from cooking the fish and keep whisking until the sauce comes to a boil. Simmer 2 minutes, then add salt and pepper to taste and stir in the cream. Add the parsley and spoon the sauce over the fish and vegetables; serve at once.

Entreé

Tourtière de Boeuf

2 lb chuck steak
$\frac{1}{2}$ lb beef kidneys
$\frac{2}{3}$ cup flour seasoned with salt and pepper
2 cups well-flavored stock
$\frac{1}{2}$ lb mushrooms
1 egg, beaten to mix (for glaze)

For the pastry
3 cups flour
pinch of salt
4 tablespoons lard or shortening
$\frac{3}{4}$ cup butter
2 egg yolks mixed with $\frac{1}{3}$ cup ice cold water

8-inch diameter springform pan

Method
Set the oven at 350°F.

Cut the steak into one-inch pieces and cut the kidneys into bite-sized pieces and roll both in the $\frac{2}{3}$ cup of flour. Pack them into an ovenproof casserole, pour in the stock, cover tightly and cook in the preheated oven for $1\frac{1}{2}$ hours or until both are very tender. Leave to cool completely.

For the pastry: sift the flour and salt into a bowl and cut in the lard or shortening and butter until you have small flour-coated pieces. Then rub them in with your fingertips until the mixture resembles breadcrumbs. Tip the yolks and water into the flour and mix quickly with a knife to form a dough. If necessary, add a few drops more of water to make a mixture that comes together easily.

Turn dough onto a lightly floured board and knead gently; wrap in plastic film and refrigerate for 30 minutes before using to make the pie.

Wash, trim and quarter the mushrooms. Preheat the oven to 400°F.

Roll out $\frac{2}{3}$ of the pastry and line the springform pan. Put the steak and kidney mixture into the dough a spoonful at a time, adding the quartered mushrooms as you do this. Roll out the remaining pastry to form a lid for the pie and brush it with beaten egg. Decorate the edge with any pastry trimmings, and brush them with glaze also. Refrigerate the pie for 1 hour.

Set the pie on a baking sheet and bake it for 45 minutes. Take from the oven and leave until cooled.

To freeze Release the sides of the mold and set the pie in the freezer until frozen solid. Then wrap in a double thickness of foil and return to freezer.

Thawing and serving Leave the pie in the refrigerator for 24 hours to thaw completely. Preheat the oven to 350°F. Set the pie on a baking sheet and reheat for 40–50 minutes or until a skewer inserted into the center of the pie is hot to the touch when withdrawn. Cut into wedges for serving with potato, beet and apple salad.

Accompaniment to entrée

Beet, Potato and Apple Salad

2 fresh beets
3 medium potatoes
2 dessert apples
vinaigrette dressing made with 2 tablespoons vinegar, salt and pepper, dry mustard and a generous $\frac{1}{3}$ cup oil
salt and pepper

Method
Trim the beets and, without peeling them, put them into a saucepan with cold water to cover. Bring to a boil, cover and simmer for 25–35 minutes or until they are tender when pierced with a skewer.

Meanwhile put the potatoes into a saucepan with cold water to cover and boil steadily for 20 minutes or until they are tender when pierced.

When the beets are ready, drain them and rinse with cold water until cool enough to handle. Slip their skins off and discard them. Dice them on a plate into half-inch cubes.

When the potatoes are ready, drain them and while still hot, peel off their skins. Dice the flesh into quarter-inch cubes.

Peel, quarter and core the apple and dice the flesh. Pile the apple, beets, potatoes into a bowl and pour in the vinaigrette dressing. Add salt and pepper to taste and refrigerate until serving.

After the springform mold has been lined with pastry, fill it with the steak and kidney mixture, then cover with pastry lid

Coupes d'Ananas

1 large pineapple
$\frac{1}{4}$ cup sugar syrup or
2 tablespoons sugar
2 tablespoons kirsch

For parfait mixture
1 cup heavy cream
2 egg whites
$\frac{1}{2}$ cup sugar

6 coupe glasses

Method

Carefully cut the skin from the pineapple. Split the pineapple in half lengthwise and slice one half into six $\frac{1}{4}$-inch thick slices. With a small round cutter, stamp out the core and put the pineapple into a container. Sprinkle it with the sugar syrup or dust it with the sugar. Cover and freeze.

With a fork, shred the flesh from the other pineapple half, discarding the core, and reserving the juice for another recipe. Put the flesh into a bowl.

For the parfait mixture: whip the cream until it holds a soft shape. Then beat the egg whites and when they are stiff, add the sugar a tablespoon at a time. When the mixture forms stiff peaks, fold in the cream, and then fold in the crushed pineapple. Return to the freezer container and cover; freeze.

Thawing and serving Remove pineapple slices from the freezer several hours before serving; keep in refrigerator. One hour before serving, transfer parfait mixture from freezer to refrigerator. Spoon the parfait mixture into 6 chilled coupe glasses with an ice cream scoop and top each one with a pineapple slice. Sprinkle over some of the kirsch and serve.

A choice of petits fours

Miroirs

1 cup ground almonds
$\frac{2}{3}$ cup sugar
1 tablespoon apricot jam glaze (see box)
1 vanilla bean
1 egg white
1 egg, beaten to mix
pinch of salt
$\frac{1}{2}$ cup slivered almonds, finely chopped

To finish
about $\frac{1}{4}$ cup apricot jam glaze
$\frac{1}{4}$ cup pistachio nuts, halved

Makes 18.

Method

Set the oven at 350°F. Grease and flour a baking sheet.

Pound and bruise the ground almonds with the end of a rolling pin and beat in the sugar a little at a time. Add the apricot jam glaze and a couple pinches of vanilla scraped from inside the bean. Beat the egg white with a fork and add it a few drops at a time to the mixture, adding only enough to make a firm paste which you can mold with your hand.

Roll the dough in your palms into small balls the size of walnuts. Mix the beaten egg with the pinch of salt and roll each almond ball in the beaten egg, then into the chopped almonds. Use a fingertip to make an indentation in each ball and set them in rows on the baking sheet. Bake in the preheated oven for 10–12 minutes or until golden brown.

Leave the miroirs to cool and when cold, fill hollows with apricot jam and set the pistachio halves around.

Soleils

For ovals
$\frac{2}{3}$ cup ground almonds
$\frac{1}{3}$ cup sugar
1 heaping teaspoon flour
$1\frac{1}{2}$ tablespoons butter, at room temperature
1 egg yolk
$\frac{1}{2}$ teaspoon rum
1 egg white (optional)
$\frac{1}{4}$ cup apricot jam glaze (to finish)

For filling
1 egg white
$\frac{1}{2}$ cup ground almonds
$\frac{1}{4}$ cup sugar

Pastry bag and $\frac{1}{4}$-inch plain round tip

Makes 20.

Method

Set oven at 350°F. Butter and flour a baking sheet.

For the ovals: pound the ground almonds with the sugar and flour. Beat in the soft butter, yolk, rum and stir well. If the mixture is a little dry, moisten it with a few drops of the optional egg white. The mixture must be soft enough to pipe.

For the filling: beat the egg white until stiff, then stir in the almonds and sugar.

Put the first mixture into the pastry bag and pipe ovals on the baking sheet, making them about $2\frac{1}{2}$-inches long. Put the second mixture into the bag and pipe it into the center of the ovals.

Bake the petits fours in the preheated oven for 8–10 minutes or until lightly browned. Take them from the oven and brush the centers with the apricot jam glaze. Leave until completely cool.

Apricot jam glaze
Put the contents of 1 jar of apricot jam into a saucepan with the juice of $\frac{1}{2}$ lemon and $\frac{1}{4}$ cup water. Bring to a boil, stirring, and simmer for 5 minutes. Strain and return to the pan. Boil another 5 minutes and store in the original jar. To use immediately: continue boiling until the glaze is very thick, then brush over cakes or petits fours. If you use a smooth jam (with no lumps of fruit), water is not needed.

A freezer menu

Left: the finished tourtière. Front: the dessert, a kirsch-flavored pineapple ice, ready to serve with a choice of petits fours

Chicken mexicain, sautéed in butter with wine and onion, is then set on a mixture of corn, rice and more onion

QUICK DISHES FOR THE BUSY COOK

In this section we offer you recipes for main courses which can be put together with relatively little preparation. These simple dishes, when combined with a fresh fruit or fruit salad, or cheese for dessert, give you quite elegant menus. They can also be used on those days when you find yourself with unexpected guests. Some of these dishes can be prepared partially in advance, and those guidelines are marked within each recipe.

All of them serve six unless otherwise stated.

CHICKEN PIECES

Five of the following recipes use chicken pieces. Look over the packages of parts carefully to see that all the legs on one tray, for instance, are very nearly the same size. Then, before using them, make sure the backbone is trimmed away from all thighs, quarters or breasts.

Recipes in this section serve 6, unless otherwise stated.

Arborio is an Italian rice which absorbs more liquid than regular rice and comes out very creamy, typical of the classic Italian risottos. It should not be washed before cooking.

Chicken Mexicain

6 large chicken breasts
3 tablespoons butter
1 large white onion, sliced
1 cup white wine
$1\frac{1}{2}$ cups long grain white rice, cooked
1 can (1 lb) corn kernels, drained
salt and pepper

Method

Dry the chicken breasts on paper towels. Melt 2 tablespoons of the butter in a skillet and sauté the chicken breasts, skin side down, until they are golden brown. Shake the pan while cooking to prevent the chicken from sticking. Take the chicken from the pan and put in the onion. Cover and cook for 5 minutes or until soft but not brown. Pour in the white wine and boil steadily until it is reduced by half. Replace the chicken in the pan, flesh side down, cover and cook gently for 20 minutes or until chicken is not quite done. Set the oven at 350°F.

Take the chicken breasts from the pan and reduce the juices until they are thick and syrupy. Add the remaining 1 tablespoon of butter to the pan, add the cooked rice and stir with a fork over the heat. Add the corn with salt and pepper to taste; stir well.

Butter a baking dish and spoon the rice and corn into it. Arrange the chicken on top, season with salt and pepper and cover with the lid. Cook in the preheated oven for 15 minutes or until the chicken is done. Serve with a green salad.

Chicken Sauté Paprika

6 large chicken pieces
3 tablespoons flour
1 teaspoon paprika
3 tablespoons butter
$1\frac{1}{4}$ cups tomato sauce (see page 91)
1 small jar pimiento caps
salt
$\frac{3}{4}$ cup light cream
1 teaspoon arrowroot
1 tablespoon cold water

For serving
8 oz noodles
$\frac{1}{4}$ cup shredded almonds
2 tablespoons butter

Method

Dry the chicken pieces on paper towels and roll them in the flour and sprinkle with the paprika.

Melt the butter in a skillet and brown the chicken on the skin side only. Turn over and pour in the tomato sauce and the juice from the pimientos. Add salt, bring to a boil, cover and simmer gently for 30–35 minutes. Shred and add pimientos to the chicken with the cream. Stir carefully.

For serving: cook the noodles in plenty of boiling salted water until just 'al dente'. Meanwhile fry the almonds in the butter until golden brown. Toss the drained noodles with the almonds and keep warm.

Mix the arrowroot to a paste with the water and pour into the chicken. Shake the pan to distribute the thickener and serve with the noodles.

Chicken en Casserole Dijonnaise

6 large chicken pieces
2 strips bacon
2 tablespoons butter
1 shallot, finely chopped
$1\frac{1}{2}$ tablespoons flour
$1\frac{1}{4}$ cups chicken stock
bouquet garni
salt and pepper
2 tablespoons heavy cream
1 tablespoon Dijon-style mustard
1 tablespoon chopped parsley

Method

Preheat the oven to 350°F. Dry the chicken pieces with paper towels. Cut the bacon into $\frac{1}{2}$-inch strips. Melt the butter in a flameproof casserole, put in the chicken pieces skin side down and brown slowly first on one side and then the other. Take them from the pan and add the bacon strips and shallot and continue cooking until both are golden brown. Blend in the flour and cook another couple of minutes until the flour is straw-colored. Add the stock and bring to a boil, stirring, then add the bouquet garni, salt and pepper and replace the chicken pieces. Cover and cook in the preheated oven for 30–35 minutes or until the chicken is cooked.

Remove the bouquet garni, skim any fat on the surface of the sauce and stir in the cream. Taste the sauce for seasoning, take the pan from the heat and arrange the chicken pieces on a platter. Whisk the mustard and parsley into the sauce and spoon over the chicken; serve at once.

Watchpoint Do not let the sauce come to a boil after the mustard has been added or it will spoil the delicate flavor.

Chicken Reginiello

6 large chicken pieces
1 tablespoon butter
½ cup dry white vermouth
2 sprigs tarragon or pinch dried tarragon
salt and pepper

For sauce
2 tablespoons butter
2 tablespoons flour
1¼ cups milk
3 oz Reginiello cheese, grated or ½ cup grated Cheddar mixed with Parmesan
2 tablespoons heavy cream
1 tablespoon browned crumbs (to finish)

Method

Preheat the oven to 350°F. Pat the chicken dry with paper towels. Melt the butter in a flameproof casserole and cook the chicken, skin side down, until it is not quite browned. Turn the pieces of chicken over, pour on the vermouth, add the tarragon, salt and pepper and bring to a boil. Cover and cook in the preheated oven for 35 minutes or until the chicken is done.

Meanwhile, prepare the sauce: melt the butter and stir in the flour. Cook 1 minute, then blend in the milk. Bring to a boil, stirring, and simmer 2 minutes. Add salt and pepper to taste and press a piece of waxed paper directly onto the surface of the sauce. Preheat the broiler.

Arrange the chicken on a flameproof platter and keep warm. Stir the hot vermouth from cooking the chicken into the white sauce and return the sauce to the boil. Take from the heat, stir in the cheese and cream and spoon the sauce over the chicken.

Sprinkle the chicken with the browned crumbs and slide under the broiler to brown.

Chicken Sauté Chasseur

6 large chicken pieces
3 tablespoons flour seasoned with salt and pepper
3 tablespoons butter
1 cup white wine
¼ lb mushrooms, finely sliced
1 shallot, finely chopped
1 tablespoon tomato paste
1¼ cups demi-glace sauce (see Vol 21)
salt and pepper

Method

Dry the chicken pieces with paper towels. Dust each piece with the seasoned flour. Melt 2 tablespoons of the butter in a skillet and brown the chicken slowly on the skin side. Turn the pieces over and pour in half the white wine. Bring to a boil, cover and simmer for 10 minutes.

Meanwhile, melt the remaining 1 tablespoon butter in a saucepan, add the mushrooms and stir over a high heat until they start to brown. Add the shallot and cook another minute. Pour in the remaining ½ cup white wine and simmer until the liquid is reduced by half. Whisk in the tomato paste and the demi-glace sauce and simmer for 5 minutes.

Pour the sauce over the chicken pieces in the pan and shake the pan gently to mix the sauce with the chicken cooking liquid. Continue simmering gently for 15 minutes or until the chicken is cooked. Taste for seasoning and serve garnished with croûtes of fried bread.

Poussins Farcis aux Raisins

To serve 4

4 Cornish hens
1 cup raisins
½ cup sherry
1 medium onion, finely chopped
1½ tablespoons butter
4 strips bacon

For pilaf
1 medium onion, chopped
2 tablespoons butter
1 cup Italian Arborio rice
1 tablespoon tomato paste
2½–3 cups chicken stock
1 bay leaf
salt and pepper

Method

Combine the raisins and sherry in a bowl and leave to soak for at least 15 minutes, or as long as 2 hours. Set the oven at 350°F.

Cook the onion in the butter, add the raisins and sauté 1 minute. Put the onion and raisin mixture inside the birds and secure the legs closed with string or poultry pins. Halve the bacon and lay 2 short strips on each bird.

For the pilaf: soften the onion in the butter in a large flameproof casserole. Cook until beginning to brown, then add the rice and cook until it begins to stick to the pan. Add the tomato paste with 2½ cups of the stock and stir well until the mixture comes to a boil.

Put the Cornish hens on the rice, tuck in the bay leaf, sprinkle everything with salt and pepper and cover with the lid. Cook the hens in the preheated oven for 15 minutes, then take off the lid, raise the heat to 400°F, and continue cooking for another 15 minutes or until the chickens are cooked and the bacon is crisp. Add more stock during cooking if the rice seems dry.

Discard the bay leaf before serving.

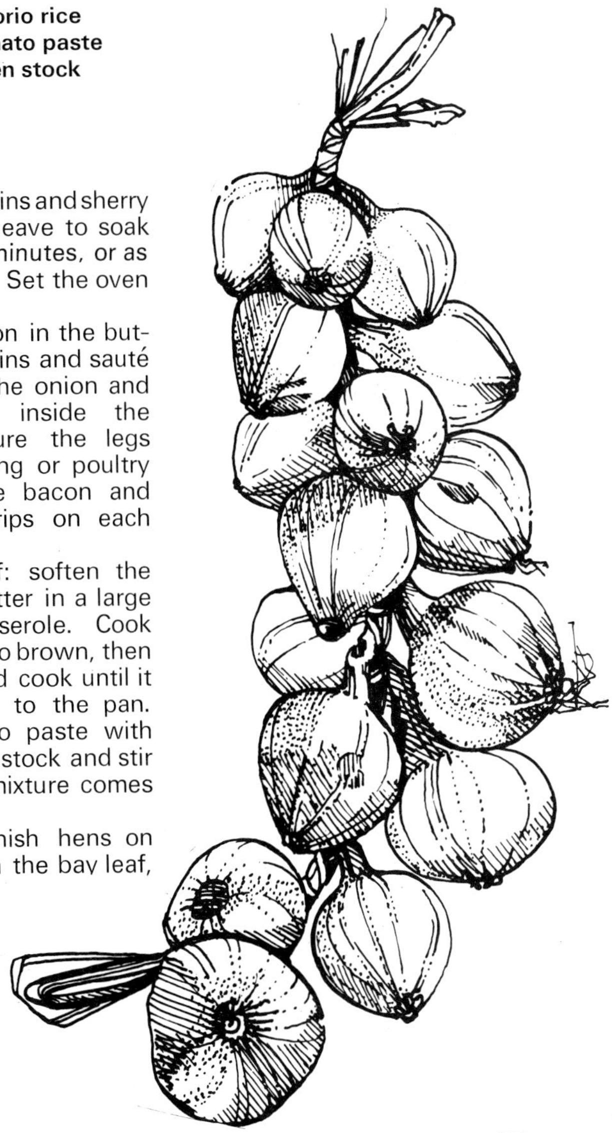

THINLY CUT STEAKS

Since beef is so expensive now, many supermarkets sell thinly cut steaks. If frozen, they defrost quite quickly and when patted dry with paper towels, will fry very nicely. Heavy-based frying pans produce the best pan-fried steaks. Use as little oil as possible (just enough to keep the butter from burning) and fry the meat over a very high heat. Deglaze the juices in the pan and pour those over the meat as a sauce. Here are a couple more ideas.

Steaks with Mushroom Salpicon

To serve 4

4 thinly cut steaks (about 6 oz each)
1 tablespoon oil
3 tablespoons butter
1 medium onion, finely chopped
1 lb mushrooms, sliced
dash of anchovy essence
salt and pepper
3 tablespoons cream
1 tablespoon chopped parsley

Method

Heat the oil in a heavy-based skillet until hot. Add $1\frac{1}{2}$ tablespoons of the butter and when foaming, brown the steaks over a high heat, first on one side and then the other. Take from the pan and arrange on a platter; keep warm.

Add the remaining butter to the pan and cook the onion for 2 minutes. Add the mushrooms and sauté until the mushrooms release their liquid. Continue cooking over a high heat until the mushroom liquid is almost evaporated, then stir in the anchovy essence, salt and pepper and cream. Continue cooking until this liquid almost disappears, then spoon it over the steaks. Sprinkle with the chopped parsley and serve at once.

Steak Paupiettes

6 thinly cut steaks (about 6 oz each)
$\frac{3}{4}$ lb loose sausage meat
1 egg, beaten to mix
1 tablespoon chopped parsley
4 strips bacon
2 tablespoons oil
4 large onions, cut into rings
1 cup well-flavored brown stock
salt and pepper
1 teaspoon arrowroot mixed with 1 tablespoon cold water

Method

Spread the steaks on the work surface and make the stuffing: mix the sausage meat with the beaten egg and chopped parsley. Divide the mixture among the steaks and roll them up. Secure them with string or toothpicks. Set the oven at 350°F. Cut bacon into $\frac{1}{2}$-inch strips.

Heat a heavy-based flameproof casserole and add the oil. When hot, put in the paupiettes and brown carefully on all sides. Lift them out, lower the heat and add the bacon and onion rounds. Cook gently until the bacon and onions are both golden brown. Discard any extra fat in the pan and set the paupiettes right in the onions so they are completely covered.

Pour in the stock with salt and pepper to taste and bring to a boil. Cover and cook in the preheated oven for 40 minutes or until the paupiettes are very tender, turning them over once or twice.

Lift out the paupiettes and onion mixture with a slotted spoon and set in a dish; keep warm. Boil up the cooking liquid and let it reduce for 5 minutes. Then whisk in the arrowroot paste, taste for seasoning and spoon over the paupiettes; serve at once.

Steak with Spiced Zucchini

To serve 4

4 thinly cut steaks (about 6 oz each)
salt and black pepper
1 medium zucchini
2 shallots, finely chopped
4 tablespoons butter
$\frac{1}{2}$ teaspoon paprika
$\frac{1}{2}$ teaspoon ground cumin
2 tablespoons wine vinegar

Method

Grind some black pepper onto each steak and set aside.

Peel the zucchini, scoop out the seeds and cut the flesh into strips the size of your little finger. Put the shallots and 2 tablespoons of the butter in a skillet and cook until soft but not brown. Add the paprika and ground cumin and cook another minute, then add the zucchini with salt and pepper to taste. Sauté the mixture for 5 minutes, then pour in the vinegar, cover the pan and simmer an additional 5 minutes. Adjust the seasoning and pour the mixture onto a warm platter; keep warm.

Wipe out the pan with paper towels and add the remaining 2 tablespoons butter. When hot, fry the steaks on both sides until browned. Arrange the steaks on the vegetable mixture, pour over any juices from the pan and serve at once.

Quick-to-make dishes

Thinly cut steak is topped with a mushroom salpicon

Trout with Asparagus and Rich Cream Sauce

To serve 4

4 rainbow trout, boned without splitting
salt and pepper
1 lb fresh asparagus
1 cup white wine
2 egg yolks
$\frac{2}{3}$ cup light cream
1 tablespoon chopped parsley

Method

Butter a baking dish large enough to hold all four trout. Lay the trout on the work surface and sprinkle the inside with salt and pepper to taste. Set aside. Set the oven at 350°F.

Snap the woody stems off the asparagus and use a vegetable peeler to pare two-inches of the stem end to remove the stringy fibers.

Bring a very large saucepan of water to the boil and blanch the asparagus for 1 minute. Drain and rinse with cold water.

Divide the asparagus among the trout, tucking them inside each fish. Lay the trout in the baking dish and pour around the white wine. Sprinkle them with salt and pepper to taste and bake in the preheated oven for 35 minutes or until the trout flake easily when pierced with the tip of a knife and the asparagus are tender.

Carefully tip the liquid in the baking dish into a saucepan and boil it over a high heat to reduce it to 3 tablespoons. Meanwhile, keep the trout loosely covered in a warm place.

Put the egg yolks in a saucepan and gradually stir in the cream. When the wine has stopped boiling, gradually stir it into the yolks and then stir the sauce over a very low heat until it thickens, but do not let it boil or it will curdle. Add salt and pepper to taste and stir in the parsley. Spoon the sauce over the trout and serve at once.

Cheese and Walnut Stuffed Flounder

To serve 4

4 small whole flounder (about 10 oz each)
1 8-oz package cream cheese
$\frac{1}{4}$ cup fresh white breadcrumbs
$\frac{1}{4}$ cup coarsely chopped walnuts
2 gherkin pickles, coarsely chopped
$\frac{1}{2}$ teaspoon paprika
salt and pepper
2 tablespoons butter
1 lemon, cut into wedges
handful parsley sprigs (for garnish)

Method

Wash the flounder and cut away the fins with kitchen scissors. Put the fish on a board white side up. Cut along the length of the backbone to within 1-inch of the tail and head. Use a small sharp knife with short strokes to ease the fish from either side of the backbone to within $\frac{1}{2}$-inch of the edge. Preheat the oven to 375°F.

Soften the cream cheese in the bowl of an electric mixer until light. Add the breadcrumbs, walnuts, gherkins, paprika and salt and pepper to taste and beat well to mix.

Divide the stuffing among the prepared fish, pressing it into the pockets formed by your partial boning. Sprinkle the skin of the fish with salt and pepper.

Use the butter to grease a large roasting tin and lay in the fish. Dot them with more butter and cover with foil.

Bake the fish in the preheated oven for 20 minutes. Remove the foil, baste with the butter in the pan, and return, uncovered, for 10 more minutes or until the fish is tender. Transfer to warmed plates and garnish with the lemon wedges and parsley sprigs for serving.

Baked Halibut in Yogurt

To serve 4

2 lb boneless skinless halibut
salt and pepper
1 tablespoon oil
1 onion, chopped
4 strips bacon, cut into strips
1 small carton plain yogurt
1 tablespoon flour
2 tablespoons chopped parsley
$\frac{1}{4}$ teaspoon dried basil
$\frac{1}{4}$ teaspoon dried tarragon
$\frac{1}{4}$ teaspoon dried oregano
$\frac{1}{4}$ teaspoon dry mustard
squeeze of lemon juice
handful of parsley sprigs (for serving)

Method

Wash the halibut and pat it dry with paper towels. Butter a baking dish and set the fish in it; season with salt and pepper.

Heat the oil in a skillet and fry the onion and bacon until the bacon is crisp. Leave to cool slightly. Set the oven at 375°F.

Mix the yogurt with the flour, parsley, basil, tarragon, oregano, mustard, lemon juice and salt and pepper to taste. Lift the bacon and onion from the skillet with a slotted spoon and add to the yogurt mixture. Pour this sauce over the fish and cover with foil.

Bake the fish in the preheated oven for 35–40 minutes or until the fish flakes easily when tested with the tip of a knife. Garnish the fish with the parsley sprigs and serve at once.

Truites au Four

6 rainbow trout
$\frac{1}{2}$ cup flour seasoned with salt and pepper
4 tablespoons butter
$1\frac{1}{4}$ cups unflavored yogurt
1 tablespoon prepared horseradish
salt and pepper

Method

Set the oven at 350°F and have a large flameproof baking dish or oval skillet on hand. Trim the trout, but leave the heads and tails on. Wash and dry with paper towels. Roll each fish in seasoned flour.

Heat the butter in the flameproof dish or skillet and when foaming, drop in the fish. Fry on one side for 5 minutes, then turn carefully and fry 4 minutes on the other side. Keep the heat at a medium setting so the fish doesn't brown, but the skin becomes very crisp.

Slide the dish into the preheated oven for 5 minutes.

Meanwhile, mix the yogurt with the horseradish and salt and pepper to taste and coat the center of the fish (leave the heads and tails exposed) with this sauce. Return the fish to the oven for an additional 5 minutes. Serve at once with a beet and potato salad.

Beet and Potato Salad

4 fresh beets, trimmed
1 lb small new potatoes
vinaigrette dressing made with 3 tablespoons vinegar, salt, pepper, dry mustard, and a generous $\frac{1}{2}$ cup oil
1 tablespoon mixed chopped parsley and chives

Method

Cook the unpeeled beets by bringing them to a boil in cold water to cover and boiling steadily for 30–40 minutes or until they are tender. Slip off the skins and slice the beets thinly on a plate.

Cook the potatoes in a large pan of boiling salted water for 15 minutes or until they are tender. Peel them while they are still hot and pour over two-thirds of the dressing with the parsley and chives.

Pile the potato into a serving dish and arrange the sliced beets in a circle around the edge. Pour the remaining dressing on the beets and chill the salad until serving.

For Truites au four, the trout is coated with a sauce of plain yogurt flavored with horseradish. A beet and potato salad accompanies this.

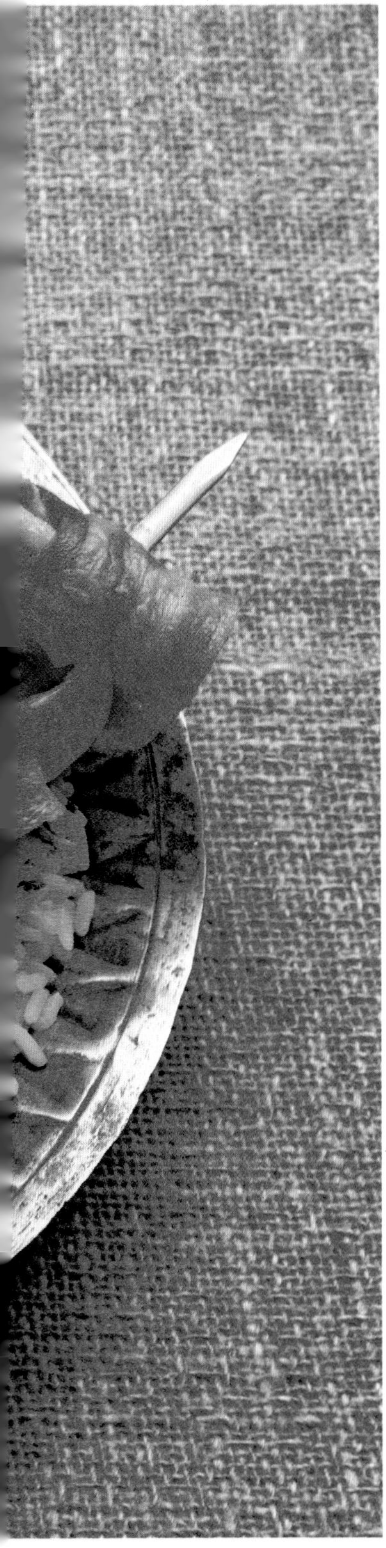

Smoked Haddock Kebabs

To serve 4

$1\frac{1}{2}$ lb boneless smoked haddock
8 strips bacon
1 red bell pepper
$\frac{1}{2}$ lb mushrooms
4 bay leaves
2 tablespoons butter, melted
juice of 1 lemon
salt and pepper
2 cups cooked rice
1 tablespoon chopped parsley
4 lemon wedges (for garnish)

Method
Cut the haddock into 16 bite-sized pieces. Halve each strip of bacon and wrap one piece around each piece of haddock.

Core, halve and seed the pepper. Cut it into 12 pieces and drop into boiling water for 1 minute; drain and rinse with cold water.

Thread the bacon-wrapped fish, pieces of pepper, and mushrooms with the bay leaves on metal skewers and sprinkle them with melted butter, lemon juice and salt and pepper to taste.

Set the skewers in a roasting pan and preheat the oven to 500°F. Cook the kebabs in the hot oven, basting with the juices that fall into the roasting pan, for 15 minutes or until all the vegetables and fish are cooked.

Arrange the kebabs on a bed of rice mixed with chopped parsley, and garnish with wedges of lemon for serving.

The skewers hold pieces of smoked haddock wrapped in bacon, alternating with bell peppers and mushrooms; they are baked in the oven and served on a bed of rice sprinkled with parsley

Striped Bass in an Indonesian Marinade

6 striped bass steaks or fillets (about $2\frac{1}{2}$ lb total)
$\frac{3}{4}$ cup sesame oil (from an Oriental market)
juice of $1\frac{1}{2}$ lemons
2 cloves of garlic, peeled and smashed
$\frac{1}{2}$ cup soy sauce
1 tablespoon ground coriander
salt and pepper

Method
Lay the fish in a large shallow flameproof baking dish and pour the sesame oil and lemon juice over them. Set the smashed cloves in the liquid and pour the soy sauce on the fish. Turn it several times in the marinade to mix the liquids together.

Sprinkle the steaks or fillets with the ground coriander and salt and pepper to taste and turn again several times.

Cover the dish loosely and refrigerate the fish for 30 minutes.

Preheat the broiler. Broil the fish in the marinade for 8–10 minutes or until the top is browned, basting occasionally with the marinade in the dish. Transfer to warm plates, discard the garlic and serve at once.

Baked Swordfish Steak

$2\frac{1}{2}$ lb thickly cut swordfish steak (in one piece)
$\frac{1}{2}$ cup soy sauce
$\frac{1}{2}$ cup oil
juice of 3 lemons
$\frac{1}{2}$ cup white wine
salt and pepper

Method
Set the swordfish in a large baking dish. Whisk the soy sauce, oil, lemon juice, white wine and salt and pepper together and pour this over the fish. Leave to marinate for 20 minutes.

Set the oven at 500°F. Bake the fish right in the marinade, basting several times during cooking, for 30 minutes or until it flakes easily when tested with a knife.

Serve the swordfish with a cherry tomato and watercress salad.

Cheese Crumb Flans

1 cup cracker crumbs (such as trisquits)
2 tablespoons grated Jarlsberg, Gruyère or Swiss cheese
$\frac{1}{4}$ cup butter, melted
salt and pepper
1 teaspoon Dijon-style mustard

$8\frac{1}{2}$-inch diameter ovenproof flan dish

Method

Set the oven at 350°F. Mix the cracker crumbs with the cheese in a bowl and stir in the melted butter, salt and pepper, and mustard. Press the mixture into the bottom and sides of the flan dish with the back of a spoon.

Bake the crust in the preheated oven for 10 minutes, then leave to cool. Fill the flan with either of the following suggestions and serve with a seasonal salad.

Note: the crumb crust can be baked and then frozen, if liked.

Egg, Pimiento and Tomato Filling

5 tablespoons butter
1 onion, finely chopped
2 cloves garlic, crushed
4 ripe tomatoes, scalded, peeled, seeded and coarsely chopped
salt and pepper
3 caps (one jar) pimiento, shredded
3 eggs, beaten to mix
3 tablespoons heavy cream
1 tablespoon chopped parsley

Method

Melt half the butter and cook the onion and garlic until soft but not brown. Add the chopped tomatoes to the pan and season with plenty of salt and pepper. Turn up the heat and cook rapidly until most of the water evaporates.

Take the pan from the heat and add the remaining butter, shredded pimiento, eggs and cream. Return to a very low heat and continue cooking, stirring slowly, until the mixture thickens creamily. Turn the eggs into the prebaked crumb crust and sprinkle with the parsley. Leave to cool completely before cutting into wedges for serving.

Savoury Ham and Cheese Filling

$1\frac{1}{4}$ cups velouté sauce (made with $1\frac{1}{2}$ tablespoons butter, $1\frac{1}{2}$ teaspoons paprika, $1\frac{1}{2}$ tablespoons flour, $\frac{1}{2}$ cup chicken stock and $\frac{1}{2}$ cup milk
2 egg yolks
$\frac{1}{4}$ cup grated Cheddar cheese
salt and pepper
$\frac{1}{2}$ envelope unflavored gelatin soaked in 1 tablespoon water
$\frac{1}{3}$ cup heavy cream, softly whipped
1 egg white
$\frac{1}{2}$ cup boiled ham, cut into shreds
1 tablespoon chopped parsley

Method

Make velouté sauce and add paprika to the melted butter before stirring in the flour. While the sauce is still hot, take from the heat and stir in the egg yolks. Return to the heat and stir until the yolks are cooked, but do not let the sauce boil. Beat in the grated cheese with salt and pepper to taste and stir in the soaked gelatin until it dissolves.

Leave the sauce to cool, then stir it over a bowl filled with ice cubes and when it is on the point of setting, remove from ice and fold in the whipped cream. Beat the egg white until it holds a stiff peak and fold it into the mixture with the shredded ham and parsley. Pour into a pre-baked crumb crust and leave in the refrigerator for $\frac{1}{2}$ an hour or until set. Cut into wedges for serving.

Cheese and Olive Flan

For the pastry
$1\frac{1}{2}$ cups flour
pinch of salt
4 tablespoons butter
2 tablespoons solid vegetable shortening
1 egg yolk
3 tablespoons ice water

For filling
12-oz container dry curd cottage cheese
1 cup light cream
$\frac{1}{2}$ cup grated Cheddar cheese
2 eggs, beaten to mix
$\frac{1}{2}$ cup black olives, pitted and halved
$\frac{1}{2}$ lb boiled ham, shredded
salt and pepper

9-inch diameter flan ring

Method

For the pastry: sift the flour with the salt. Rub in the butter and shortening until the mixture resembles breadcrumbs. Mix the egg yolk with the ice water and stir it into the flour until the mixture comes together to form a dough. Knead lightly on a floured board and add a few drops more water if necessary. Wrap the pastry in plastic film and refrigerate 15 minutes.

For the filling: beat the cottage cheese and cream in an electric mixer and beat in the Cheddar cheese and the eggs, a little at a time. Stir in the olives and ham and add salt and pepper to taste.

Set the oven at 375°F. Roll the pastry to a large round and line it into the flan ring set on a baking sheet. Prick the bottom in several places and pour in the filling. Bake the flan in the preheated oven for 30–40 minutes or until set in the middle. After 20 minutes' cooking, lift off the flan ring carefully and return the tart to the oven until completely done. Take out when cooked, and leave until cool. Refrigerate for two hours or until cold and cut into wedges for serving.

This cheese crumb flan base has a filling of egg, pimiento and tomato. Flan cases like this one are easy to make and can be frozen until required. Make a batch by increasing the ingredients and trying your own fillings

SALPICONS FOR PILAFS

The salpicons given here are intended for quickly prepared lunch or supper dishes. Classically speaking, a salpicon is a mixture of any shredded or finely cut ingredients that are bound with a white or brown sauce and used as a garnish or filling for pastry cases. The recipes that follow use salpicons as mixtures that are folded into cooked rice or served along with it. All leftovers lend themselves to easily prepared salpicons, so if you're pressed for time, substitute what you have on hand for the ingredients combined below.

Basic Pilaf

$1\frac{1}{2}$ cups long grain white rice
1 medium onion, finely chopped
6 tablespoons butter
3–$3\frac{1}{2}$ cups chicken stock
salt and pepper
$\frac{1}{2}$ cup grated Cheddar cheese

Method
Set the oven at 350°F. In a heavy-based flameproof casserole, cook the onion in the butter until soft but not brown. Add the rice and cook for a couple of minutes or until the grains begin to look transparent. Pour in 3 cups of the stock with salt and pepper to taste and bring to a boil. Cover and cook the rice in the preheated oven for 15 minutes. Check that the rice still has some liquid left in the pan and add a little more if necessary. Without fluffing rice, recover; return to the oven for 5–7 minutes or until tender.

Dust the cheese on the top of the rice and set it to one side of the stove for 5 minutes. Then turn the grains carefully with a fork and serve with one of the following;

Steak and Tomato Salpicon

$1\frac{1}{2}$ lb flank steak
3 tablespoons butter
$\frac{1}{3}$ cup Marsala
2 medium onions, finely sliced
$\frac{1}{4}$ lb mushrooms, quartered
1 tablespoon flour
1 tablespoon tomato paste
1 cup stock
1 bay leaf
1 clove of garlic, crushed
salt and pepper
4 tomatoes, peeled and halved

Method
Halve the flank steak lengthwise and lay both halves on a baking sheet and put it into the freezer for 40 minutes or until the outside feels firm. Then slice the meat on an extreme diagonal so you have short thin strips.

Heat the butter in a large skillet and toss the strips, half at a time, over a high heat until the outside looks done. Pile all the meat in the pan and pour in the Marsala; flame it. Take out the meat and add the onions. Cook them for a few minutes, then add the mushrooms and sauté for a few minutes more.

Sprinkle the flour into the pan and continue stirring the ingredients until the flour is completely mixed in. Add the tomato paste and stock with the bay leaf, garlic and salt and pepper to taste. Replace the meat, bring to the boil, cover and simmer gently for 15 minutes.

Cut the seeded tomato halves into strips and stir them into the steak mixture. Serve at once with rice pilaf.

Chicken and Pepper Salpicon

3 lb roasting chicken
1 onion, quartered
1 carrot, sliced
1 stalk of celery
bouquet garni
salt
6 peppercorns

For salpicon
1 large onion, thinly sliced
3 tablespoons butter
1 heaping tablespoon flour
1 cup stock from cooking chicken
2 green bell peppers, cored, seeded and cut into shreds
salt and pepper
$\frac{2}{3}$ cup light cream

Method
Put the chicken into a large saucepan or kettle and add the onion, carrot and celery. Pour in enough cold water to come level with the top of the thighs and bring slowly to the boil. Skim the scum that rises to the surface and add the bouquet garni, salt, peppercorns and cover with the lid. Lower the heat and poach the chicken for about 1 hour or until tender. Cool the chicken in the liquid and reserve the stock.

Skin the bird and pull the meat from the bones. Shred the meat into two-inch pieces and set them aside.

For the salpicon: soften the onion in the butter for a couple of minutes.

Stir in the flour and cook until the flour begins to turn a pale straw-color. Pour in the chicken stock and bring to a boil, stirring. Simmer 2 minutes.

Meanwhile, drop the peppers into a saucepan of boiling water and cook 1 minute; drain and refresh with plenty of cold water. Add the peppers and shredded chicken to the sauce and season with salt and pepper to taste. Return to the boil, add the cream, and stir well. Cook for 5 minutes over a low heat.

Arrange the rice pilaf in a large circle around the edge of a platter and spoon the chicken inside. Serve at once.

Smoked Haddock, Bacon and Mushroom Salpicon

$\frac{3}{4}$ lb boneless smoked haddock fillet
$\frac{1}{2}$ cup each milk and water
$\frac{1}{2}$ lb Canadian bacon
4 tablespoons butter
1 medium onion, thinly sliced
$\frac{1}{2}$ lb mushrooms, sliced
salt and pepper

Method
Put the fish in a skillet and pour in the milk and water. Bring just to a boil, then cover with the lid and remove the pan from the heat. Leave on the side of the stove for 15 minutes. Meanwhile, remove any rind on the bacon and cut it into slices, then across each slice into strips.

Drain the fish and break it apart into flakes with two forks.

Melt 3 tablespoons of the butter in a skillet and fry the onion and bacon for 5 minutes or until they just begin to turn brown.

Add the remaining 1 tablespoon butter to the pan with the mushrooms and continue cooking for 3 minutes, stirring occasionally. Add salt and pepper to taste and stir in the haddock.

Fork in the rice pilaf and pile into a bowl for serving.

COOKING IN A STUDIO APARTMENT

The lack of space, both for storing and preparing food, is often a major drawback for a studio apartment dweller. But even in the smallest of kitchens, it is possible to make a simple, elegant dinner for two.

A dry white wine, such as the Italian Orvieto Secco or a Californian Dry Semillon, would make a good partner for either choice of appetizer and for the main course, too, and turn the occasion into something special . . .

Ham Roulades
or
Bean and Pineapple Salad

Zucchini and Bacon Omelet
Crisp Green Salad

Cold Layered Apple and Gingersnap Fool
or
Hot Apple and Gingersnap Pudding

White wine – Orvieto Secco (Italy)
or Dry Semillon (California)

TIMETABLE

Day before
Make salad dressing and store in a jar.
Make cold apple fool and refrigerate without decoration.
Or, prepare hot apple pudding but do not bake.
Cut bacon and zucchini for omelets and refrigerate covered.

Evening
Prepare salads but do not dress. Make ham roulades.
Decorate cold apple fool just before serving.
Or, put hot apple pudding in oven 20 minutes before dinner.
Make omelets at the last minute, keeping first omelet in a warm place, covered with an inverted bowl, while making the second.

We tend to skip preparing an appetizer when pressed for time, opting instead to serve a green salad first. Here are a couple of ideas that take no more effort than a green salad, but are a little more interesting.

Ham Roulades

8 thin slices of boiled ham
$\frac{1}{8}$ lb sliced cooked tongue
small can (about 5 oz) liver pâté
1 teaspoon Dijon-style mustard
salt and pepper
few sprigs parsley (for garnish)

Method
Lay the slices of ham on a board. Cut the tongue into fine shreds and mix it into the liver pâté with the mustard and salt and pepper to taste. Spread some of this mixture on each slice of ham and roll them up. Place the roulades side by side on a small platter and cover with waxed paper and a wet paper towel until ready to serve.

Serve, garnished with parsley as an appetizer with brown bread and butter.

Bean and Pineapple Salad

1 can (about 1 lb) pineapple chunks in their own juice
$\frac{1}{2}$ lb green beans
$\frac{1}{2}$ lb mushrooms
$\frac{1}{3}$ cup oil, or to taste
juice of $\frac{1}{2}$ lemon
salt and pepper
1 tablespoon chopped parsley
1 tablespoon chopped chives mixed with chopped fresh mint

Method
Drain pineapple and set aside. Trim the green beans and cut them into one-inch diamond-shaped pieces. Drop into boiling water, return to the boil and cook steadily for 3 minutes. Drain, refresh and drain again.

Wipe mushrooms and slice them thickly. Put the mushrooms in a bowl and slowly pour on the oil until all the mushrooms are coated with it. Add the lemon juice with salt and pepper to taste, the parsley, chives and mint. Stir in the drained pineapple and green beans and mix well. Chill the salad for 1 hour and serve as an appetizer with crusty bread and butter.

Zucchini and Bacon Omelet

6 tablespoons butter
4 thin slices Canadian bacon, cut into dice
1 medium zucchini, thinly sliced
4 eggs
2 tablespoons water
salt and pepper
3 tablespoons freshly grated Parmesan cheese
few sprigs of watercress or parsley (for garnish)

7-inch omelet pan

Method

Heat 2 tablespoons of the butter in a skillet and sauté the bacon and zucchini until they begin to brown. Keep warm.

Beat the eggs with the water and salt and pepper to taste.

Heat 2 tablespoons of the butter in the omelet pan and, when foaming, add half the egg mixture. Stir the edges into the center while the eggs cook over a gentle heat and when the bottom of the omelet is set but not brown, add half the zucchini mixture and fold the omelet in half. Slide it onto a plate and cover with an inverted bowl to keep warm.

Make the second omelet in exactly the same way. Sprinkle the finished dishes with the cheese and garnish them with the watercress or parsley. Serve at once.

Cold Layered Apple and Ginger Snap Fool

2 cooking apples, peeled, cored and sliced
3 tablespoons water
1 tablespoon granulated sugar
3 tablespoons butter
1 tablespoon light brown sugar
12 ginger snaps, crushed to make crumbs
3 tablespoons plain yogurt
1 dessert apple (optional)

Method

Put the cut up cooking apples in a saucepan with the water, and granulated sugar and cook over a low heat until the liquid is very hot. Cover the pan and continue cooking, stirring occasionally, for 15 minutes or until the apples are pulpy. Turn into a bowl to cool.

Melt the butter in the saucepan and stir in the brown sugar. Add the crushed ginger snaps and mix well. Leave to cool.

Fold the yogurt into the apple purée and layer it with the ginger snaps in two glasses, beginning and ending with ginger snaps. Refrigerate until ready to serve.

If decorating, do so just before serving: halve the dessert apple and cut it into thin slices. Arrange overlapping on each glass and serve at once.

Hot Apple and Ginger Snap Pudding

2 cooking apples
2 tablespoons butter
grated rind and juice of $\frac{1}{2}$ lemon
$\frac{1}{4}$ cup light brown sugar
12 ginger snaps, broken up
1 small container sour cream

6-inch soufflé dish or small casserole

Method

Set the oven at 350°F. Butter the soufflé dish or small casserole.

Peel, core and cut the apples right into a skillet. Add the butter and fry the apples quickly over a fairly high heat until completely coated with butter. Add the lemon rind and juice, sprinkle over the sugar and stir well to mix.

Arrange a layer of half the crushed cookies in the bottom of the soufflé dish, add half the apples and cover with half the sour cream. Continue with the remaining ingredients and cover the dish with foil. Bake in the preheated oven for 30 minutes. Serve at once.

A simple but elegant supper for two: zucchini and bacon omelets accompanied by crunchy salads and served with white wine. To follow, there's a cold apple and gingersnap fool

NEW WAYS WITH VEGETABLES

A handful of beautifully cooked green beans is always appropriate beside the entrée, but sometimes the occasion calls for a heartier or more interesting vegetable preparation. If the main course is roast chicken or capon, some broiled steak or a baked fish, accompany it with one of these unusual vegetable dishes. Or serve a vegetable entrée with a salad for a light supper. That idea, once regarded as unusual or the prerogative of vegetarians, is becoming increasingly more acceptable.

How to prepare vegetables for baking

1 Peel or scrub root vegetables and if they vary in size, cut them so they are all fairly even.
2 Cook root vegetables in enough boiling salted water to just cover for 8 minutes. Then drain and dry on paper towels.
3 Cook soft vegetables, such as peppers or summer squash in boiling water for 2 minutes or until just softened. Drain and dry on paper towels.
4 To bake root vegetables, melt enough drippings or oil in a roasting pan to make a thin layer on the bottom and add the vegetables when the fat is hot – it should sizzle.
5 Put roasting pan into a preheated 400°F oven and cook them for 15 minutes or until the bottoms are browned. Turn vegetables over and cook another 10 minutes. Then pour the fat out of the pan and continue cooking the vegetables until tender.
6 To bake soft vegetables: follow individual recipes. Most stuffed green vegetables will need no liquid in a lightly buttered pan; some, such as artichokes or stuffed cabbage, will need a generous layer of liquid.

Vegetables for Baking
Beans: Dried beans, which have been soaked overnight, are often cooked in the oven in a covered casserole.
Beets: Small whole beets, rubbed with oil or sitting in some liquid, can be baked.
Cabbage: Whole leaves can be blanched, used as a wrapper for various fillings, and baked. Shredded cabbage is also suitable for oven cooking with liquid in the casserole.
Carrots: Rub with butter or oil and bake whole.
Corn on the cob: Rub with butter and bake in a covered pan with water and milk.
Globe artichokes: Boil until soft enough to remove hairy chokes, then stuff and bake until tender; or halve and lay in a dish with olive oil and bake.
Eggplant: Bake whole, halved, or stuffed.
Jerusalem artichokes: trim and bake whole.
Mushrooms: Bake whole, quartered or stuffed.
Onions: Bake whole stuffed.
Parsnips: Quarter and rub with oil and bake.
Peppers: Blanch bell peppers and stuff before baking.
Potatoes: Bake after scrubbing, then stuff and return to the oven; or peel and roast whole small potatoes.
Pumpkin: Cut into wedges, rub each with oil and bake.
Squash: Summer squash can be baked after stuffing; winter squash is suitable for baking after halving and discarding seeds.
Sweet potato: Bake whole or sliced.
Tomatoes: Bake whole, halved or stuffed.
Turnips: Bake small ones whole after blanching.

Eggplant Baked with Ham

4 medium eggplants
salt and pepper
½ cup oil
2 tablespoons butter, at room temperature
4 large tomatoes, scalded, peeled and thinly sliced
¼ lb Mozzarella cheese, thinly sliced
⅓ lb boiled ham, finely chopped
¾ cup heavy cream
¼ cup fresh white breadcrumbs
¼ cup freshly grated Parmesan cheese

Method

Trim the eggplants and cut them into slices. Pile them in a colander, sprinkling each layer with salt. Leave for 30 minutes to drain. Rinse the eggplant and pat them dry with paper towels. Set the oven at 375°F.

Heat enough oil in a skillet to make a thin film on the bottom and fry some of the eggplant until lightly browned. Continue frying eggplant until they are all done. Use the butter to generously grease a baking dish.

Put a layer of eggplant in the bottom of the dish and sprinkle with salt and pepper. Add a layer of tomatoes, then Mozzarella cheese, then sprinkle on some ham. Pour over a little cream and continue layering the ingredients, ending with all the remaining cream.

Mix the breadcrumbs with the Parmesan cheese and cover the dish with it. Bake the eggplant in the preheated oven for 45 minutes, or until a skewer inserted into the center of the dish is very hot to the touch when withdrawn. Slide the dish under the broiler for 1 minute just to brown the top and serve at once.

Stilton Baked Leeks

1 bunch (4 large) leeks
2 tablespoons butter
2 tablespoons flour
½ cup white wine
¾ cup milk
salt and pepper
½ lb Stilton cheese, crumbled
4 large slices Virginia ham
1 tablespoon Dijon-style mustard
2 large tomatoes, scalded, peeled and thinly sliced

Method

Wash and trim the leeks and if they are very sandy, soak the green ends down in a large bowl of cold water to rid them of their grit. Drop the leeks into boiling salted water and cook for 5 minutes. Drain and rinse with cold water.

Set the oven at 400°F. Grease an ovenproof dish large enough to hold the leeks.

Melt the butter in a saucepan, stir in the flour and cook until the flour begins to turn a pale straw color. Pour in the wine and milk and bring to a boil, stirring constantly; simmer 2 minutes. Add salt and pepper to taste and stir in all but a couple tablespoons of the cheese until it melts.

Spread the slices of ham with the mustard and wrap a slice around each leek. Arrange them in the baking dish and spoon over the sauce. Sprinkle with the remaining crumbled cheese and arrange the tomatoes in rows on top. Bake in the preheated oven for 20 minutes or until the sauce is bubbling at the edge. Serve at once.

Finish Eggplant baked with ham with a thick sprinkling of breadcrumbs and Parmesan cheese

Baked Vegetable Kebabs with Spicy Sauce

1 large eggplant, peeled and cubed
8 small firm tomatoes, quartered
2 medium onions, peeled and quartered
1 red bell pepper, cored, seeded and cut into squares
1 green bell pepper, cored, seeded and cut into squares

For sauce
$\frac{1}{4}$ cup soy sauce
$\frac{1}{4}$ cup sherry
1 teaspoon prepared horseradish
1 teaspoon Dijon-style mustard
1 tablespoon honey

Method
Bring a saucepan of water to the boil and drop in the cubes of eggplant. Boil steadily for 3 minutes, then drain and pat dry.

Thread the eggplant on skewers with the tomatoes, onions, and red and green peppers. Lay the skewers in a roasting pan and set the oven at 350°F.

For the sauce: whisk the soy sauce, sherry, horseradish, mustard and honey together and brush the kebabs generously with the sauce. Lift the skewers so the ends sit on the rim of the roasting pan.

Bake the kebabs for 25 minutes, basting frequently with the sauce, or until the vegetables are tender. Serve at once.

Nut-stuffed Cabbage Leaves

3 tablespoons oil
1 small onion, finely chopped
$\frac{1}{4}$ lb bacon, cut into fine strips
1 cup pine nuts (from a specialty market)
$\frac{2}{3}$ cup long grain white rice
salt and pepper
$\frac{1}{2}$ teaspoon dried tarragon
$\frac{1}{4}$ teaspoon dried thyme
1 tablespoon chopped parsley
1 medium firm green cabbage
$1\frac{1}{4}$ cups chicken stock

Method
Heat 1 tablespoon of the oil in a skillet and fry the onion until soft but not brown. Add the bacon and cook until it is crisp. Drain all but 1 tablespoon of the oil from the pan. Stir in the pine nuts and cook for 1 minute. Set aside.

Bring a large saucepan of water to the boil and add the rice. Return the water to the boil and cook the rice steadily for 12 minutes. Butter a shallow baking dish and set the oven at 350°F.

Drain the rice at once into a colander and poke several holes in the rice with the end of a wooden spoon.

Stir the rice into the bacon mixture with salt and pepper to taste, the tarragon, thyme and parsley. Set aside.

Blanch the whole head of cabbage in boiling water for 1 minute, then peel away as many leaves as you can before re-blanching. Peel away 8 large leaves altogether.

Lay the cabbage on a board and remove the stalk (see Vol 7). Place $\frac{1}{8}$ of the filling in the center of the leaf and roll up the cabbage like a small package.

Set the cabbage in the baking dish and continue rolling the other leaves in the same way, setting them in the dish as close together as possible to keep them from unrolling.

Heat the chicken stock with the remaining oil until boiling and pour it into the dish at the edges. Add enough water so the liquid just covers the rolls and cover with a lid or foil.

Bake in the preheated oven for 40 minutes or until a skewer inserted into the cabbage is hot to the touch when withdrawn, and the cabbage leaves are very tender. Serve at once.

Crusty-Topped Carrots

$1\frac{1}{2}$ lb carrots
2 eggs
3 tablespoons milk
salt and pepper
$\frac{1}{3}$ cup flour
2 tablespoons butter
$\frac{1}{4}$ cup freshly grated Parmesan cheese

Method
Trim and scrape the carrots and cut them into finger lengths. Pile into a saucepan with water to cover and bring to a boil. Cook steadily for 3 minutes.

Set the oven at 350°F and butter an ovenproof dish.

Beat the eggs and milk together in a bowl. Add salt and pepper to the flour and put it on a plate.

Dip the carrots into the egg mixture, lift them out with a fork one at a time and coat them with the flour. Arrange them in the baking dish and dot with the butter. Sprinkle with the cheese and bake in the preheated oven for 45 minutes or until crusty and very tender. Serve at once.

Stir-fried Broccoli with Water Chestnuts

1 bunch broccoli
1 can (6 oz) water chestnuts, drained
1 inch-long piece of ginger root, peeled
2 tablespoons peanut oil
2 tablespoons dry sherry
2 tablespoons water
salt and pepper

Method
Use a paring knife to peel the stems on the broccoli, discarding any leaves as you move down the stalks. Trim a slice from the bottom of each stalk and cut the remaining spear into 1-inch lengths on the diagonal. Pile them on a plate with the flowerets.

Halve the water chestnuts and halve the ginger.

Have all the remaining ingredients on hand.

Heat the oil in a heavy-based skillet and when very hot, add the ginger and cook for 1 minute. Add the broccoli and water chestnuts and stir fry over high heat until they have absorbed the oil.

Add the sherry and water and bring to a boil. Cover the skillet and cook the mixture over a high heat for 2 minutes, or until the broccoli is tender when pierced with a skewer. Add salt and pepper to taste, discard the ginger, pile the vegetables in a heated serving dish and serve at once.

Lemon-Baked Corn

4 ears fresh corn
grated rind and juice of 1 lemon
4 tablespoons butter, melted
1 tablespoon chopped parsley
salt and pepper

Method

Set the oven at 375°F. Discard the husks and silk from the corn and break off the stem. Wash the cobs and dry with paper towels.

Put the lemon rind and juice in the bottom of a heatproof shallow dish just large enough to hold the corn. Add the melted butter, parsley and salt and pepper. Turn the corn in the mixture until they are well coated, then bake the corn in the preheated oven for 35 minutes, basting with the juices in the pan frequently, until the corn is tender. Serve at once.

Deliciously buttery Lemon-baked corn is sprinkled with parsley and needs frequent basting during the cooking time

A variety of baked stuffed potatoes with their different fillings – see recipes at right

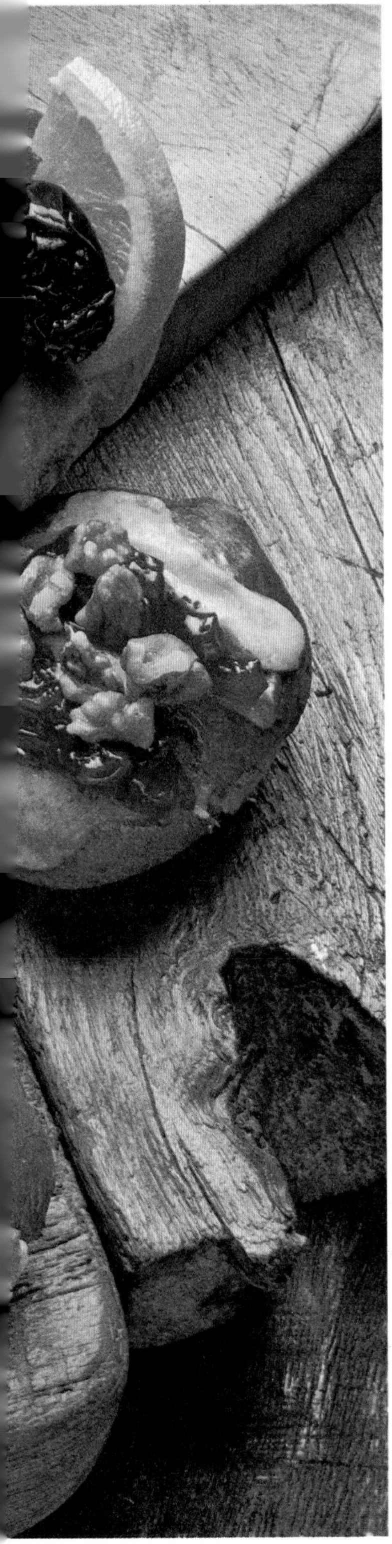

STUFFED POTATOES

A baked potato is such a natural container for a myriad of stuffings that restaurants serving only spuds have opened in several cities recently. Here is the basic recipe for baked potatoes and some lovely additions.

Set the oven at 400°F. Scrub potatoes (choose a baking variety such as Idaho or Russet) with a vegetable brush. Prick once or twice and set them directly on the rack in the preheated oven and bake for 1 hour, or until tender when pierced with a skewer. Slit and stuff.

Cheese and Bacon

Scoop potato out of the skin and for each one mix 2 tablespoons grated Cheddar cheese, 1 tablespoon butter, and salt and pepper to taste. Return to skin and garnish with 3 strips of bacon, rolled tightly, skewered onto a toothpick and broiled crisp.

Danish Potato

Scoop potato out of the skin and for each one mix 1 tablespoon chopped parsley with 1 slice cooked pork, finely chopped. Pile up in potato and garnish each with a half slice of orange, a prune and some cooked red cabbage.

Sausage Potato

Slash potato and fill with 1 sliced onion sautéed in 2 tablespoons oil until soft. Skewer a slice of broiled sausage, tomato, broiled sausage, an onion ring and a sprig of parsley. Add to potato.

Cheese and Chutney Potato

Cut potato three-quarters of the way through at $\frac{1}{2}$-inch intervals. Squeeze sides of potato and place a little chutney into each cut. Put a triangle of Swiss cheese into each cut so that it melts slightly and garnish along the center with walnut pieces.

Ham and Pineapple

Slash potato with a cross on top and pinch in sides slightly. Into each potato place a few pineapple chunks and some cubed ham with a tablespoon of butter. Garnish each potato with a small roll of thinly sliced ham and a pineapple slice. Top with a sprig of parsley.

Sour Cream Dressing

For each potato, mix together $\frac{1}{4}$ cup sour cream with a squeeze of lemon juice and salt and pepper to taste. Add 1 tablespoon chopped chives or spring onion tops. Slash a cross on top of each potato and pinch in sides slightly. Pour in the dressing and garnish with a spring onion whose top has been cut like a brush.

Pizza Potatoes

Cut a cross on top of potato and pinch in the sides slightly. Into each potato, place some cubes of Mozzarella and a sprinkling of oregano. Put a wedge of tomato in the cross and garnish with a lattice of anchovies and a black olive.

Bolognaise Potato

For leftover spaghetti or meat sauce: cut a deep slash in the top of the potato, pinch the sides in slightly and fill the slash with the meat sauce. Sprinkle with plenty of freshly grated Parmesan cheese.

Deviled Potato

For each potato, cook a small half of kidney or one chicken liver in a little oil with a few slices of onion. When cooked, add a dash of Worcestershire sauce and Tabasco sauce with salt and pepper to taste. Cut a deep slash in each potato and fill with the onion mixture. Tuck two rolled and broiled slices of bacon into the slash with the kidney or chicken liver.

Scotch Woodcock Potato

Slash potato across center and fill each one with some creamy scrambled eggs. Garnish with a fillet of anchovy and some capers.

Seafood Potatoes

Cut a cross on top of each potato and pinch the sides slightly. Fill each potato with some steamed mussels, cover with a creamy sauce and some grated cheese and garnish with one large shrimp.

Baked Artichokes with Shrimps

4 medium artichokes
$\frac{1}{2}$ lemon
$\frac{1}{2}$ lb cooked shrimps
$\frac{1}{2}$ cup fresh white breadcrumbs
$\frac{1}{2}$ cup Parmesan cheese
$\frac{1}{4}$ cup chopped parsley
salt and pepper
3 tablespoons butter
3 tablespoons flour
$1\frac{1}{2}$ cups milk

Method

Trim the stalks, tops and leaves of each artichoke, rubbing all cut surfaces with the lemon as you do so. Drop them into a large pan of boiling salted water, cover, and cook them for 20 minutes.

Drain artichokes upside-down on a plate.

Mix the shrimps, breadcrumbs, Parmesan cheese, parsley and salt and pepper in a bowl. Preheat the oven to 350°F.

Melt the butter in a saucepan, stir in the flour and blend in the milk. Cook, stirring, until the sauce comes to a boil; add salt and pepper and simmer 2 minutes; stir in the shrimp mixture.

Remove the hairy chokes from the artichokes and divide the filling among them. Set the artichokes in a buttered baking dish and cook them for 30 minutes or until a skewer inserted into the artichokes is hot to the touch when withdrawn. Serve at once.

The cooked artichoke is filled with shrimps in a creamy sauce, flavored with cheese and parsley

Almond Duchesse Potatoes

4 medium potatoes, peeled and in a bowl of cold water
salt and pepper
4 tablespoons butter
about 12 whole blanched almonds, halved

Pastry bag and large star tip

Method

Quarter the potatoes and put them into a saucepan with cold water to just cover. Bring to a boil, cover and simmer for 15 minutes or until the potatoes are tender.

Drain potatoes and work them through a ricer or food mill into a bowl. Beat in salt and pepper to taste with the butter. Fill the pastry bag with the potato mixture. Leave to cool until comfortable to handle.

Set the oven at 400°F and lightly butter a baking sheet.

Pipe about 24 large rosettes of potato onto the baking sheet and garnish each one with an almond half pressed into the top. Bake the potatoes in the preheated oven for 15 minutes or until pale golden brown on top. Serve at once.

Italian Potatoes

4 medium potatoes, boiled and mashed (but still hot)
4 tablespoons butter
1 onion, finely chopped
1 green pepper, cored, seeded and chopped
1 small red pepper, cored, seeded and chopped
2 tablespoons flour
2 eggs
salt and pepper
1 tablespoon chopped parsley
1 can (1 lb) whole tomatoes, drained
1 teaspoon dried oregano

Method

Melt half the butter in a skillet and sauté the onion and peppers for a few minutes. Add half of them to the mashed potatoes with the remaining butter and beat well. Set skillet with vegetables aside. Stir in the flour and eggs with salt and pepper to taste. Beat in the parsley and taste for seasoning.

Set the oven at 375°F and butter an ovenproof dish.

Lightly flour a board and pat the potato mixture out on it into an inch-thick round that is the same size as the dish.

Arrange the round in the baking dish, and bake it in the preheated oven for 25 minutes, or until lightly browned.

Meanwhile, add the tomatoes to the vegetables left in the skillet, crush them with the back of a fork and add plenty of salt and pepper to taste. Stir in the oregano, bring to a boil, and cook uncovered for 5 minutes.

Arrange the potato cake on a serving dish and spoon over the tomato mixture. Serve at once.

Fan Potatoes

Peel one potato per person and put them into a saucepan with cold water to cover. Bring to a boil and cook 8 minutes. Drain and dry on paper towels. Cut potatoes across into slices but do not cut right through. Brush each potato with 1 tablespoon melted butter and set them in a roasting pan. Bake in preheated 400°F oven for 30-40 minutes or until they are golden brown and crusty. Serve at once.

Zucchini Provençales

6 medium zucchini, trimmed and cut into 2-inch slices
1 small onion, finely chopped
$\frac{1}{4}$ cup olive oil
4 medium tomatoes, scalded and peeled
salt and pepper
$\frac{1}{2}$ cup grated Parmesan cheese

Method

Fry the zucchini slices and onion in 3 tablespoons of the oil over a high heat for several minutes, shaking the contents of the pan as they cook. Take out and set aside.

Set the oven at 350°F and lightly butter a baking dish.

Halve the tomatoes and seed them; cut the halves into thick strips. Heat the remaining 1 tablespoon oil in the skillet and cook the tomatoes gently for a few minutes.

Layer the zucchini and tomatoes in the baking dish, sprinkling each layer with salt and pepper. Dust the top with the grated cheese and bake the dish in the preheated oven for 20 minutes or until the zucchini is very tender. Serve at once.

Zucchini Milanese

8 zucchini
$\frac{1}{4}$ lb boiled ham, chopped
2 tablespoons chopped parsley
1 tablespoon dried oregano
2 tablespoons fresh wholewheat breadcrumbs
$\frac{1}{2}$ cup grated Cheddar cheese
2 eggs
2 tablespoons butter
1 tablespoon flour
$\frac{3}{4}$ cup milk
salt and pepper

Method

Trim the zucchini and drop into a large saucepan of boiling water; cook for 5 minutes, then drain.

Halve each zucchini lengthwise and scoop out the pulp. Pile it into a bowl and reserve the shells.

Set the oven at 375°F and lightly butter a baking dish large enough to hold the eight zucchini halves. Arrange them in the dish.

Add the ham, parsley, oregano, breadcrumbs, all but 3 tablespoons of the cheese, and the eggs to the pulp in the bowl. Stir well.

Melt the butter in a saucepan, stir in the flour and cook 1 minute. Blend in the milk, stirring constantly, until the mixture comes to a boil; lower the heat and simmer 2 minutes. Add salt and pepper to taste.

Refill the shells with the ham mixture, mounding them well. Coat each zucchini with a little of the sauce and dust the tops with a sprinkling of the reserved cheese. Bake in the preheated oven for 30 minutes or until lightly browned on top. Serve at once.

Lemon-Braised Zucchini

3 medium zucchini
$\frac{3}{4}$ cup water
grated rind and juice of 1 lemon
salt and pepper
2 tablespoons freshly chopped parsley

Method

Trim the zucchini and slice them thickly; set aside. Put the water into a saucepan with the grated lemon rind and juice. Bring to a boil and add salt and pepper to taste. Add the zucchini and simmer for 3 minutes or until the zucchini are just done, turning them in the liquid from time to time. Transfer the zucchini to a serving dish, cover and keep in a warm place.

Reduce the cooking liquid until it is only 2 tablespoons and stir in the parsley. Spoon this over the zucchini and serve at once.

Mushrooms au Gratin

$1\frac{1}{2}$ lb small mushrooms
4 tablespoons butter
1 onion, finely chopped
1 cup sour cream
1 tablespoon chopped fresh chives or spring onion (scallion) tops
2 tablespoons flour
$\frac{1}{2}$ cup grated Gruyère cheese
2 tablespoons fresh white breadcrumbs

Method

Melt the butter in a large skillet and fry the mushrooms and onion over a high heat for a few minutes. Transfer the mushrooms with a slotted spoon to a 9-inch baking dish. Set the oven at 400°F.

Stir the sour cream, chives or onions and flour into the skillet with all but 3 tablespoons of the cheese. Spoon the sour cream mixture over the mushrooms and scatter the breadcrumbs on top. Sprinkle them with the remaining cheese and bake the dish in the preheated oven for 35 minutes or until bubbling at the edges. Serve at once.

Mushrooms baked in sour cream make a superb supper dish; or try serving it as an accompaniment to broiled or baked swordfish steaks

Cauliflower Aurore

1 large head cauliflower
$1\frac{1}{4}$ cups milk
1 slice of onion
1 slice of carrot
pinch dried thyme
1 bay leaf
salt and pepper
2 tablespoons butter
$1\frac{1}{2}$ tablespoons flour
$\frac{1}{4}$ cup tomato sauce (see page 91)
paprika (for sprinkling)

Method

Cut the core from the cauliflower and divide the head into flowerets. Bring a large saucepan of water to the boil and drop in the sprigs. Simmer for 8 minutes or until the sprigs are just tender. Drain and set aside.

Set the oven at 200°F and lightly butter a small heatproof bowl.

Bring the milk to scalding point with the onion, carrot, thyme, bay leaf and salt and pepper. Leave to infuse for 10 minutes, covered.

Melt the butter in a saucepan and stir in the flour. Cook for 1 minute, then take from the heat and strain in the milk; whisk well to blend it thoroughly, then return to the heat and bring to a boil, stirring. Simmer for 2 minutes, then add the tomato sauce and taste for seasoning.

Arrange the cauliflower sprigs in the bowl, stalks ends facing toward the center, and cover with foil. Press another small bowl right onto the cauliflower and leave it in the preheated oven for 5 minutes.

Turn out the cauliflower mold onto a small round platter. Bring the sauce just back to a boil and spoon it over the mold. Dust with paprika and serve at once.

Cauliflower Toscana

1 large head of cauliflower
3 tablespoons butter
1 teaspoon chopped chives or spring onion (scallion) tops
$\frac{1}{4}$ lb mushrooms, chopped
1 cup vegetable stock
salt and pepper
2 egg yolks
$\frac{1}{3}$ cup light cream
1 tablespoon arrowroot
2 slices of bread, toasted
1 tablespoon chopped parsley

Method

Cut the core from the cauliflower and divide the head into flowerets. Bring a large saucepan of water to the boil and drop in the sprigs. Simmer for 6 minutes or until they are not quite tender. Drain and return them to the saucepan with $1\frac{1}{2}$ tablespoons of the butter, the chives or onions, mushrooms, vegetable stock and salt and pepper to taste. Bring to a boil, cover and simmer for 2 minutes.

Mix the egg yolks with the cream and arrowroot and set aside.

Arrange the slices of toast in a deep serving dish and lift out the cauliflower sprigs and set them on the toast. Cover with foil and keep warm.

Return the vegetable stock to a boil and stir a few tablespoons of it into the egg yolks. Whisk the yolks back into the stock and return almost to the boil. Take the sauce from the heat, add the remaining $1\frac{1}{2}$ tablespoons butter, whisk well and taste for seasoning. Spoon the sauce over the cauliflower, sprinkle with the parsley and serve at once.

Piquante Beets

1 bunch (about 5 small) fresh beets
2 tablespoons vinegar
1 teaspoon salt
1 tablespoon sugar
pepper
1 tablespoon butter

Method

Trim the beets and put them into a saucepan with water to just cover. Bring to a boil and cook steadily, covered, for 30 minutes or until the beets are tender. Drain and rinse with cold water until cool enough to handle. Then slip off the skins and discard them.

On a plate, cut the beets into dice and put them into a saucepan (not aluminum) with the vinegar, salt, sugar and pepper. Cook for a few minutes over a gentle heat until the sugar has dissolved and the liquid has absorbed the flavors of the seasonings. Take from the heat and beat in the butter a little at a time. Taste for seasoning, correct if necessary and serve at once.

Beets with Capers

1 bunch (about 5 small) fresh beets
2 tablespoons butter
salt and pepper
1 teaspoon sugar
grated rind and juice of 1 lemon
1 tablespoon chopped chives or spring onion (scallion) tops
1 tablespoon chopped parsley
2 tablespoons capers

Method

Trim the beets and put them into a saucepan with water to just cover. Bring to a boil, and cook steadily, covered, for 30 minutes or until the beets are tender. Drain and rinse with cold water until cool enough to handle. Then slip off the skins and discard them.

On a plate, dice the beets and put them into a saucepan (not aluminum) with the butter. Add the salt, pepper, sugar, and lemon rind and shake the pan over a gentle heat until the sugar dissolves. Add the lemon juice, chives or spring onions, parsley and capers and cook them just to heat everything until very hot. Pile into a serving dish and serve at once.

Lima Beans Alla Romana

4 cups shelled fresh lima beans or 2 packages (10-oz each) frozen baby limas
3 tablespoons butter
1 medium onion, finely chopped
1 tablespoon dried sage
1 can (1 lb) whole tomatoes, coarsely chopped on a plate
$\frac{3}{4}$ cup water
salt and pepper

Method
Melt the butter in a flameproof casserole and cook the onion for a few minutes until it is soft, but not brown. Add the sage and tomatoes and bring to a boil. Cook the tomatoes for 10 minutes, stirring occasionally over a gentle heat, until they are a pulp. Stir in the water and return to a boil. Add the beans, cover, and cook gently for 15–20 minutes for fresh limas or 10 minutes for frozen limas or until they are tender. Add plenty of salt and pepper to taste and serve at once.

Mélange of Braised Vegetables

2 carrots, trimmed
6 small stalks of celery, trimmed
2 medium onions
$\frac{1}{2}$ lb green beans
2 tablespoons butter
salt and pepper
2 tablespoons water
2 tablespoons chopped parsley

Method
Peel carrots and cut them into quarter-inch slices on the extreme diagonal, starting at the thin end. Do the same with the stalks of celery.

Put the carrots in a very large pan of water and bring to a boil. Drop in the celery and return the water to the boil. Cook for 2 minutes, then drain and rinse with cold water.

Set the oven at 325°F. Bring the saucepan of water to the boil again.

Meanwhile, halve the onions and slice them from root to stem into strips. Trim the beans and cut them in half on the extreme diagonal. Drop the beans into the boiling water, let the water return to the boil and cook 2 minutes. Drain and rinse with cold water until the beans turn bright green again.

Melt the butter in a flameproof casserole and cook the onions for 1 minute. Add the carrots and celery with salt and pepper to taste and stir well. Pour in the water, bring to a boil, cover and cook in the preheated oven for 10 minutes.

Stir in the green beans, cover and continue cooking for another 10 minutes or until all the vegetables are tender but still have some bite to them. Sprinkle with the parsley and serve at once.

Baked Butternut Squash

2 butternut squash
1 tablespoon oil
4 tablespoons butter, melted
$\frac{1}{4}$ cup honey
$\frac{1}{4}$ cup walnut halves
$\frac{1}{4}$ cup raisins
$\frac{1}{4}$ teaspoon ground cinnamon
pinch ground nutmeg
salt and pepper

Method
Set the oven at 350°F. Halve the squash lengthwise, remove the seeds and rub the oil on the skins. Set them in a roasting pan flesh side up and brush them with butter.

Put a tablespoon of honey into each cavity and divide the walnuts and raisins among them. Sprinkle each with cinnamon, nutmeg and salt and pepper. Bake for 1 hour or until tender when pierced with a skewer. Serve at once with brown bread and butter.

Our picnic-for-one choice – Chicken and mushroom pie, Coleslaw, and Orange and almond gingerbread

EATING OUT OF DOORS

There are many occasions when we enjoy eating in the open air – maybe we like to vary the routine by taking a picnic snack to the park. Perhaps you are planning a more elegant picnic party, or a barbecue for a summer evening? This section gives you menus for three such occasions.

The second menu is a more elegant picnic, on the theory that it's always more fun to carry food along to a beautiful spot when the weather is warm enough to enjoy the outdoors. Our menu will leave all the guests happily satisfied.

And for the barbecue menu – and some ideas on the drinks to serve with the food – turn to page 51.

PICNIC FOR ONE

For the times when you want to treat yourself to a special occasion, go off by yourself for a long walk in the country, and take yourself on a picnic on a glorious, warm sunny day, here is the menu to accompany your whim. On the theory that you should treat yourself as well as you treat your guests, we have opted for some very special choices. Some of the recipes that follow will yield more than you might want to bring along, so you'll have some left over for another day's lunch.

Chicken and Mushroom Pie

Makes three 4-inch pies

1 large (¾ lb) whole chicken breast, cooked and cooled
1 tablespoon oil
1 small onion, peeled and chopped
1 (¼-inch thick) slice of Canadian bacon, diced
¼ lb mushrooms, quartered
1 tablespoon flour
¼ cup milk
1 teaspoon chopped parsley
pinch dried thyme
salt and pepper
1 egg, beaten to mix (for glaze)

For pastry
1 cup flour
pinch of salt
4 tablespoons butter
3 tablespoons shortening
1 egg yolk mixed with 1 tablespoon ice water

3 individual flan rings or pie pans (4 inches in diameter)

Method

For the pastry: sift the flour and salt into a bowl. Rub in the butter and shortening until the mixture resembles breadcrumbs. Stir in the yolk mixture and work to form a dough. Knead lightly on a floured board and wrap in plastic film; chill for 15 minutes.

Meanwhile, discard skin and bones from the chicken and dice meat.

Heat the oil in a skillet and fry the onion and bacon for 3 minutes. Add the mushrooms and stir over a fairly high heat for another minute.

Stir the flour into the pan, then gradually pour in the milk and stir until the mixture comes to a boil. Simmer 2 minutes, then remove from the heat and stir in the diced chicken, parsley, thyme and salt and pepper to taste. Leave to cool completely.

Divide the pastry into 6 pieces. Roll each piece out into a round and use 3 to line the flan rings or pie pans. Divide the filling between the pans and cover with the other rounds. Pinch the edges all around to seal the pastry and decorate with leaves made from the trimmings. Brush the pieces with beaten egg to glaze them and make a small hole in the center of each one. Refrigerate for 15 minutes.

Set the oven at 400°F. When the oven is hot, bake the pies for 40 minutes or until the pastry is browned on top and a skewer inserted into the center is very hot to the touch. Leave the pies to cool completely, then refrigerate up to three days.

Note: Freeze the other pies by wrapping in foil; then leave in refrigerator half a day to thaw before serving.

Coleslaw with Raisins and Walnuts

thin wedge of firm white cabbage, shredded
1 carrot, shredded
1 spring onion (scallion), thinly sliced
¼ cup mayonnaise
juice of ½ lemon
pinch of sugar
salt and pepper
2 tablespoons raisins
1 tablespoon coarsely chopped walnuts

Method

Pile the cabbage into a bowl and add the carrot, spring onion, mayonnaise, lemon juice, sugar, salt and pepper to taste, raisins and walnuts. Stir to coat all the ingredients, then taste again for seasoning. Refrigerate up to two days before serving.

Crabmeat Salad

⅓ lb fresh white crabmeat
2 tablespoons mayonnaise
1 carrot, coarsely shredded
1 stalk celery, finely chopped
½ teaspoon tomato paste
1 teaspoon chopped parsley
salt and pepper
2 leaves Boston or Bibb lettuce
3 cherry tomatoes

Method

Pick over the crabmeat with your fingers to remove any bits of shell and pile it into a bowl. Stir in the mayonnaise, carrot, celery, tomato paste and parsley with salt and pepper to taste.

Arrange the leaves of lettuce in a small container and mound the crabmeat salad in the center. Garnish with the cherry tomatoes and cover with the lid. Refrigerate up to 1 day before serving.

Dilled Cucumber Salad

1 cucumber
salt
2 tablespoons fresh dill, finely chopped or 1 tablespoon dried dill
2 tablespoons top quality white wine vinegar
pepper

Method

Without peeling it, thinly slice the cucumber on a mandoline slicer, or with a stainless steel knife. Pile the cucumber into a colander and sprinkle each layer with salt. Set a plate on top and underneath the colander and leave the cucumber for 20 minutes to drain.

Layer the cucumber in a small container with the dill, vinegar and pepper, ending with a sprinkling of the dill. Cover and refrigerate up to half a day before serving.

All salads containing mayonnaise should be carried in a cooler with an ice pack and never left in the heat longer than it takes to consume them.

To some people, there is no better eating than a tart, crisp Granny Smith apple like the one in the photograph at right. The bright, shiny Red Delicious, with the knobby base, is sweet and tender and has become America's favorite. All over New England, where they grow in abundance, the spicy, tart McIntosh apples are considered the top choice.

Orange and Almond Gingerbread

$\frac{1}{2}$ cup butter
$\frac{1}{4}$ cup light brown sugar
$\frac{3}{4}$ cup light corn syrup
$\frac{1}{4}$ cup molasses
$1\frac{3}{4}$ cups flour
1 tablespoon ground ginger
$\frac{1}{4}$ teaspoon ground nutmeg
$\frac{1}{4}$ teaspoon ground allspice
$\frac{1}{2}$ teaspoon baking soda
grated rind and juice of 1 small orange
$\frac{1}{2}$ cup milk
2 eggs, beaten to mix
$\frac{1}{2}$ cup flaked almonds

$8\frac{1}{2}$ x $4\frac{1}{2}$ x $2\frac{1}{2}$-inch loaf pan

Method

Set the oven at 300°F. Grease the loaf pan, line the bottom with a piece of waxed paper cut to fit it, and grease the paper also.

Put the butter, sugar, corn syrup and molasses in a saucepan and stir them over a gentle heat until the sugar dissolves. Remove from the heat and leave to cool.

Sift the flour with the ginger, nutmeg, allspice and baking soda. Grate the orange rind into the dry ingredients.

Add enough orange juice to the milk to make $\frac{3}{4}$ cup liquid. Stir in the eggs.

Stir the dry ingredients alternatively with the milk into the molasses mixture with a wooden spoon. Sprinkle the almonds into the bottom of the pan and pour in the gingerbread mixture.

Bake in the preheated oven for $1\frac{3}{4}$ hours or until the cake is firm to the touch and pulling away from the sides of the pan. Leave to cool slightly, then turn out to cool completely. Put the cake in an airtight container for at least 2 days before serving, then cut into 2-inch thick slices and carry along whatever amount you think suitable. Store the remaining cake in the airtight tin up to 10 days.

For an impromptu picnic for one, stop by a specialty market and purchase a small crusty French bread, a thin wedge of Brie, $\frac{1}{4}$ lb sliced German salami, a half-sour pickle, and a bar of imported Swiss chocolate with an orange or pint of strawberries for dessert. Any liquor store will have a small bottle of sparkling mineral water, a split of red wine, or a bottle of good ale. It might cost a bit for that kind of readymade luxury, but aren't you going on this expedition to pamper yourself?

AN ELEGANT PICNIC FOR SIX

Individual Mushroom Quiches

For pastry
1½ cups flour
pinch of salt
4 tablespoons butter
4 tablespoons shortening
3 tablespoons ice water

For filling
2 eggs
1 egg yolk
¾ cup light cream
salt and pepper
½ medium onion, finely chopped
1 tablespoon butter
¼ lb mushrooms, sliced
½ cup grated Cheddar cheese

8 tartlet pans or individual flan rings (3½–4 inches diameter); 4½-inch cookie cutter

Method
Prepare the pastry and chill for 15 minutes while preparing filling. Set the oven at 375°F.

For the filling: beat the eggs and yolks together with a fork, gradually stirring in the light cream and salt and pepper to taste.

Cook the onion in the butter until soft but not brown, add the mushrooms and sauté quickly over a fairly high heat for 3 minutes. Add the mushrooms to the egg mixture and stir in the cheese. Set aside.

Use the cookie cutter to stamp out rounds to fit the tartlet pans and line each one with foil and some beans. Bake blind in the preheated oven for 8 minutes or until the pastry is just set.

Remove beans and paper and divide mushroom mixture equally among the tartlet molds. Return to the oven and bake for another 15–20 minutes or until firm to the touch and golden brown. Leave them to stand for 10 minutes before removing from the tins.

Serve at room temperature or reheat for 10 minutes in a preheated oven at 300°F and pack in an insulated picnic box for carrying.

Fruit and Chicken Curry

5 lb roasting chicken
2 sprigs of fresh tarragon or ½ teaspoon dried tarragon
salt and pepper
1 tablespoon butter
4 tablespoons olive or safflower oil
1 cup chicken stock (made from the giblets)
2 ripe peaches
2 ripe dessert pears
2 bananas
1 fresh mango (if available)
½ lb fresh red or black cherries, pitted
2 tablespoons superfine sugar
juice of 1 lemon

For curry sauce
1 heaping tablespoon unsweetened grated coconut
4 tablespoons butter
1 onion, chopped
1 tablespoon grated fresh ginger root
1 teaspoon crushed coriander seeds
1 teaspoon freshly ground black pepper
1 tablespoon curry powder
1 tablespoon flour
2 cups chicken stock
1 cup heavy cream

Method
Set the oven at 375°F. Put the fresh or dried tarragon inside the chicken, add some salt and pepper and the butter. Rub the oil on the skin of the bird and set it in a roasting pan. Pour around the stock and roast the chicken in the preheated oven for 2–2¼ hours or until a skewer inserted in the thickest part of the thigh releases juices that are clear and not pink. Turn and baste the chicken as it cooks; at the end of cooking the bird should be brown and sticky. Leave to cool.

Meanwhile, prepare the curry sauce: soak the coconut in a coffee cup in enough boiling water to fill the cup and leave for 15 minutes. Melt the butter in a saucepan, add the onion and cook until soft but not brown. Add the ginger, coriander, black pepper and curry powder and cook another 3 minutes over a gentle heat to mellow the spices. Add the flour and blend in the stock and bring to a boil, stirring constantly; simmer for 30 minutes, then stir in the reserved coconut and the water it is soaking in, taste for seasoning and simmer another 5 minutes. Strain and leave to cool; refrigerate until chilled.

Peel and slice the peaches, pears, bananas and mango (if using) and place in a shallow dish with the cherries. Sprinkle with the sugar and lemon juice and cover very tightly with plastic film; refrigerate.

Cut up the chicken, without removing the skin, but discarding all the bones. The chicken should be in bite-sized pieces. Pack into a container and chill.

Whip the cream until it holds a soft shape and mix it into the chilled curry sauce with the prepared fruits. Add the chicken and arrange everything in the shallow dish. Cover tightly again with plastic film and refrigerate until ready to take to the picnic site.

Cucumber, Nut and Rice Salad

2 cups long grain white rice
2 cucumbers
salt and pepper
1 bunch spring onions (scallions)
1½ cups plain yogurt
juice of ½ lemon, or to taste
1 cup unsalted cashew nuts or almonds

Method
Bring a very large kettle of water to the boil and sprinkle in the rice. Return to the boil and cook steadily for 12 minutes or until the rice is tender. Drain and poke half a dozen holes in the rice with the end of a wooden spoon; leave for 15 minutes.

Peel the cucumbers and cut them in half lengthwise. Scoop out the seeds with the tip of a teaspoon and discard them. Quarter the halves lengthwise and slice thickly into chunks. Pile the cucumber into a colander, sprinkling each layer with salt. Press with a plate and set another plate underneath the colander. Leave for 15 minutes to drain. Dry the cucumbers on paper towels.

Trim the spring onions and slice them as thinly as possible. Stir them into the yogurt with the salt and pepper, lemon juice, nuts and cucumber. Stir in the rice with two forks and taste for seasoning. Pile into the serving bowl and cover with plastic film; refrigerate until ready to serve.

A picnic menu chosen to complement the main dish – a fruit and chicken curry

Hazelnut and Chocolate Roulade

3 eggs, separated
2 teaspoons water
$\frac{3}{4}$ cup sugar
1 cup flour
$\frac{3}{4}$ teaspoon baking powder
pinch of salt
1 cup ground hazelnuts
confectioners' sugar (for sprinkling)

For filling
6 squares (6 oz) semi-sweet chocolate
1 tablespoon water
2 egg yolks
$\frac{1}{3}$ cup unsalted butter, at room temperature

Jelly roll pan (11 x 16 inches)

Method

Set the oven at 400°F. Grease the jelly roll pan, line it with waxed paper and grease the paper. Dust it with flour, tapping out the excess.

Beat the egg yolks, water and $\frac{1}{2}$ cup of sugar in the bowl of an electric mixer until very thick and mousse-like. Set aside. Beat the egg whites until stiff and gradually beat in the remaining $\frac{1}{4}$ cup sugar until the whites are very glossy. Sift the flour, baking powder and salt together.

Fold the yolks into the whites in three batches, sprinkling some nuts and flour over the mixture before folding each portion.

Spread the mixture in the prepared pan, smooth the top with a spatula and bake in the preheated oven for 12 minutes or until firm to the touch.

Have a sheet of waxed paper on the counter dusted with confectioners' sugar. Turn the cake out onto the paper, set a damp kitchen towel on the cake and roll it up in the towel. Cover with a dry towel and leave to cool.

For the filling: melt the chocolate in the water over a gentle heat, take from the heat and beat in the yolks one by one. Beat in the butter gradually and leave to cool, stirring occasionally until thickened.

Unroll the cake carefully, spread with the chocolate and reroll. Dredge the top with confectioners' sugar and wrap in foil until ready to serve.

How to make a paper case for the Hazlenut and chocolate roll:

Use parchment paper and cut off a piece that is 17-inches by 11-inches. First fold down a $1\frac{1}{2}$-inch border on each short side and crease it into place. Then cut a slit at each corner and fold one cut piece over the other to miter the corners, securing each with a paper clip. Slide the case onto a baking sheet and brush it lightly with some melted butter. Sprinkle with flour before using.

Orange and Lemon Kugelhopf

2 tablespoons butter (for mold)
grated rind of 1 orange
grated rind of 1 lemon
1 cup butter, at room temperature
$1\frac{1}{4}$ cups sugar
3 eggs
2 cups flour
2 teaspoons baking powder
$\frac{1}{2}$ cup chopped candied peel
2 tablespoons milk
confectioners' sugar (for sprinkling)

Kugelhopf mold ($8\frac{1}{2}$-inch diameter)

Method

Use the 2 tablespoons butter to grease the mold generously. Set the oven at 375°F.

Sprinkle the inside of the mold with half the orange and lemon rind. Cream the butter and sugar together until soft and light. Beat in the eggs, one at a time, beating well after each addition.

Sift the flour with the baking powder and fold it into the creamed mixture with the candied fruit, remaining grated peel and milk.

Spoon the mixture into the prepared pan and level the top carefully. Bake the cake in the preheated oven for 50–60 minutes or until golden brown and firm to the touch. Leave the cake in the pan to cool for 5 minutes, then invert it onto a wire rack to cool completely.

Set on a piece of foil, dredge with confectioners' sugar and enclose in the foil until ready to serve.

BARBECUE FOR TEN

The wonderful smell of food cooking over coals is intoxicating for the guests awaiting it, so this menu offers the simplest of grilled meats – lamb kebabs – marinated with the Oriental flavors of soy sauce and ginger. Serve them with a pilaf, add a green salad, some homemade wholewheat rolls or baked potatoes (or both) and you have a lovely outdoor party.

The turkey kebabs (see page 52), also grilled on the coals, can help you stretch your party food to feed more friends, or you can include them just to offer an alternative. And for dessert, there is a universal favorite – a cheesecake. Decorated with an apricot purée and topped with apricot halves, it is always irresistible. Offer Sangria, a cranberry and orange punch or one of the suggestions on page 55.

TIMETABLE

Day before

1 Prepare and chill cheesecake.

2 Prepare salad ingredients and store in a plastic bag; make salad dressing and store in a jar.

3 Make marinade for meat and pour over chunks; cover and refrigerate.

4 Prepare barbecued turkey, if serving (or remove barbecued turkey from freezer and prepare kebabs when thawed.)

5 Make wholewheat rolls and store in a plastic bag.

Day of Barbecue

1 Prepare potatoes (if serving) for barbecue.

2 Thread lamb and vegetables on skewers.

3 Thread turkey on skewers (if serving).

Two hours before

Start potatoes (if serving).

1 Make sangria and/or cranberry orange punch.

2 Put rice on to cook for pilaf.

3 Toss green salad while kebabs are grilling.

Japanese Lamb Kebabs

5–5$\frac{1}{2}$ lb lamb shoulder, boned
8 medium leeks, trimmed and thoroughly washed
5 green peppers, cored, seeded and halved
4 large onions
4 cloves of garlic, crushed
4-inch piece of fresh ginger root, peeled and finely chopped
3 cups soy sauce
$\frac{1}{2}$ cup dry sherry
salt and pepper
paprika (for sprinkling)

Method

Cut the lamb into 1$\frac{1}{2}$-inch cubes. Cut white part of the leeks into 1$\frac{1}{2}$-inch lengths.

Cut the green peppers into large chunks, the same size as the meat. Cut the onions into eighths, leaving a little root on each piece to hold them together.

Put the garlic, ginger, soy sauce and sherry into a saucepan and bring just to the boil. Add plenty of salt and pepper. Lay the cubes of lamb in a large pan (not aluminum) and pour over the marinade. Leave for 30 minutes.

Alternate the lamb with the vegetables on skewers. Sprinkle lightly with paprika and grill over hot coals, basting with the liquid from marinating several times during cooking.

Arrange the pilaf on a large platter and set the skewers in rows on top. Serve at once.

Rice Pilaf

Follow the instructions on page 26 but double all the quantities given there.

Barbecued Turkey

6 turkey legs or thighs
3 tablespoons bacon fat or butter
2 large onions, chopped
1$\frac{1}{2}$ cups well-flavored stock
8 ripe tomatoes

For marinade
6 tablespoons butter
$\frac{1}{3}$ cup ketchup
$\frac{1}{4}$ cup soy sauce
$\frac{1}{4}$ cup jellied cranberry sauce
$\frac{1}{4}$ cup Worcestershire sauce
salt and pepper
2 teaspoon Dijon-style mustard
large pinch of sugar

Method

For the marinade: melt the butter and stir in the ketchup. Add the soy sauce, cranberry sauce, Worcestershire sauce, salt and pepper, Dijon mustard and sugar. Cook over a low heat until the cranberry sauce melts, then take from the heat.

Skin the turkey pieces and cut the meat from the bone into large chunks. Pile them into a bowl and pour over the marinade. Leave for 3 hours or overnight.

Melt the bacon fat or butter and sauté the onion until soft, but not brown. Lift the turkey meat from the bowl (reserving the marinade) and add to the butter. Stir for a few minutes over a high heat, then pour in the stock and bring to a boil. Simmer, covered, for 30 minutes.

Meanwhile, scald, peel and quarter the tomatoes. Thread the pieces of turkey on skewers with the tomatoes, pour over the reserved marinade and chill until ready to reheat over hot coals.

Baked Potatoes

A recipe for baked potatoes is on page 37, but if you have enough room on your barbecue grill to hold all the potatoes, wash them well and prick the skins all over. Wrap each one in foil and set them right into the hot coals; leave them for 2 hours or until they are tender when pierced with a long skewer. Cook the kebabs right over the potatoes (just before they are done) and then serve everything together.

For a barbecue outdoors on a sunny evening, serve Japanese lamb kebabs with a pilaf, a green salad and baked potatoes. To follow, there's a choice of cheesecakes – the Apricot version is shown here. A pitcher of Sangria can be served instead of the more usual cocktails

Meals outdoors

Green Salads

Although salad greens will become soggy quite quickly if you dress them too early, the washed greens will wait for several hours in a plastic bag. Remove the stems and any hard white parts of the leaves and rinse them thoroughly. Lay them in a clean kitchen towel, layering every half dozen leaves with paper towels. Roll them up in the towel and slip this into a plastic bag. Secure the top with a twist and place in the vegetable bin of the refrigerator.

Alternately, dry the washed leaves in a kitchen towel, tear the leaves into pieces, and pile the torn leaves into a plastic bag; secure the end and store in the vegetable bin. Toss with a dressing just before serving.

Garlic Cream Dressing

½ cup mayonnaise
¼ cup light cream
2 cloves of garlic, crushed
2 tablespoons oil
1 tablespoon white wine vinegar
1 tablespoon Dijon-style mustard
1½ tablespoons soy sauce

Method

Whisk the mayonnaise in a small bowl, adding the light cream in a slow steady stream. Whisk in the garlic, oil, vinegar, mustard and soy sauce and taste for seasoning.

Pour over salad ingredients just before serving.

Wholewheat Rolls

1½ cups wholewheat flour
1 tablespoon sugar
½ teaspoon salt
½ cup dry milk solids
½ envelope yeast
1¾ cups lukewarm water
3¼ cups all-purpose flour

Two 9-inch round cake pans

Method

Combine the wholewheat flour, sugar, salt, dry milk, yeast, and water in the large bowl of an electric mixer. Add ½ cup of the all-purpose flour and beat the mixture at medium speed for several minutes or until it is completely smooth. Take the beaters from the bowl and stir in the remaining flour with a wooden spoon.

Knead the dough lightly on a board, adding a little more flour if necessary to prevent it from sticking, and add a few drops of oil to the bowl. Return the dough to it, turn it all around so it is completely coated with oil, and cover with a damp cloth. Leave to rise in a warm place for 1¼ hours, or until it has doubled in bulk.

Grease the cake pans.

Turn the dough out onto a board. Divide it into twelve even-sized balls and arrange six around the edges of each pan. Cover with the damp cloth and leave them to rise for 1¼ hours or until they are almost touching each other at the sides. Meanwhile, set the oven at 400°F.

Bake the rolls in the preheated oven for 20 minutes, turn the heat down to 350°F and continue baking for 10 minutes, or until the rolls sound hollow when tapped on the bottom with the knuckles.

Turn out onto racks to cool.

Wrap in plastic bags until ready to serve.

Apricot Cheesecake

For the crust
1 cup Zweiback crumbs
2 tablespoons sugar
4 tablespoons butter, melted

For filling
2 8-oz packages cream cheese
⅔ cup sugar
2 eggs
2 tablespoons lemon juice
grated rind of 1 lemon

For topping
1 can (1 lb) apricot halves

8-inch springform pan

Method

For the crust: put the Zweiback crumbs, sugar and butter in a bowl and mix well. Set the oven at 325°F.

Press the mixture evenly on the bottom and partially up the sides of the pan. Bake for 10 minutes, then leave to cool. Do not turn the oven off.

For the filling: beat the cream cheese until soft and light. Beat in the sugar gradually, then add the eggs one at a time, beating well after each addition. Add the lemon juice and rind and mix well. Pour into the crumb crust and bake the cheesecake in the preheated oven for 1 hour or until set in the middle. Turn the oven off. Leave the cheesecake inside for an additional hour. Take out and cool.

Loosen the sides of the pan and lift them off the cheesecake. Arrange the apricot halves on top and refrigerate until serving.

Drinks for the Barbecue

When you're invited to someone's house for a late afternoon or early evening summer barbecue, the host usually uses that chance to make a pitcher of his favorite new alcoholic concoction.

Those people who have a patch of fresh mint and like bourbon, can't resist Mint Juleps. To make a pitcher of 8 drinks, combine $\frac{1}{2}$ cup sugar syrup, a large handful of mint leaves and a dozen good splashes of Angostura bitters. Chill 8 tall glasses in the freezer and, when very cold, pack them with crushed ice. Strain the mint mixture into the glasses, add a jigger of bourbon to each one and stir the contents of each glass with a tall spoon. Decorate with a sprig of mint and serve at once.

Another seasónal favorite is the Strawberry Daiquiri: for 12 drinks, blend 2 pints hulled strawberries until they form a purée. Add 2 cups frozen limeade concentrate, 24 jiggers of white rum and blend again. Stir in 12 cups of crushed ice, pour into a container and store in the freezer until ready to ladle into glasses for serving.

Rum Espressos are for the guests who love coffee and whipped cream: for each drink, pour $\frac{3}{4}$ cup freshly made chilled espresso into a tall glass. Add a jigger of rum, 2 tablespoons heavy cream and stir well. Top with a spoonful of whipped cream, dust some shaved chocolate on it and serve at once.

Tequila is becoming more and more available and here is an interesting way to use it: these are called Tequila Manhattans, and they are especially for sweet vermouth lovers. For each drink, combine 2 fl oz Tequila with 2 fl oz sweet vermouth and a good squeeze of lime juice. Add ice, a cherry and a slice of orange and serve at once.

Sangria

Pile 1 cup of hulled strawberries, a large handful of stemmed and pitted cherries, a few slices of pineapple and 1 sliced navel orange into a large pitcher or punch bowl. Add $\frac{1}{2}$ cup brandy, cover and leave for several hours.

Pour in 3 bottles of full-bodied red wine, 1 thinly sliced lemon, the juice of 2 lemons, and $1\frac{1}{2}$–2 quarts of club soda. Stir well and serve at once.

Cranberry orange punch
Pour 3 quarts cranberry juice into a punch bowl and stir in 1 quart orange juice. Add 1 sliced navel orange and two cinnamon sticks. Leave covered in the refrigerator until serving.

Sunday brunch – ham and cheese-filled Croques monsieur; Melon and orange cups with 'S' shaped shortbread cookies

SUNDAY BRUNCH FOR 10

Getting together with friends for Sunday brunch is a wonderfully pleasing way to spend a weekend morning. Usually a stack of Sunday newspapers, another pot of coffee or tea, or an early afternoon televised game can make brunch an all-day event. In case you know people who like to linger, we offer some additional recipes for bringing out with your second pot of brew.

Croque Monsieur

24 slices wholewheat bread
24 large slices Gruyère or other Swiss cheese
1 teaspoon grated nutmeg
salt and pepper
24 slices boiled ham
$\frac{3}{4}$ cup butter, at room temperature
$\frac{1}{4}$ cup oil
6 eggs, beaten to mix
bunch of watercress (for garnish)

Method

Cover 12 slices of bread with 12 slices of cheese and sprinkle them with some nutmeg, salt and pepper. Put two slices of ham on the cheese and top each one with another slice of cheese and a slice of bread.

Heat half the butter and oil together in a large skillet. Dip the sandwiches, one at a time, in the beaten eggs and fry as many as will fit into the skillet at one time, turning them over after the first side is browned. Use the remaining butter and oil to fry the other sandwiches. Halve each croque monsieur and arrange on a platter. Garnish with sprigs of watercress and serve at once.

Melon And Orange Cups

6 small ripe melons
8 navel oranges
$\frac{1}{4}$ cup sugar

Method

Cut a small slice from the top and base of each melon so they will sit without rocking when they are filled. Halve the melons, scoop out the seeds with a spoon and use a melon ball cutter to scoop out the flesh. When you can no longer make melon balls, scoop out the remaining flesh with a spoon and use for another meal.

Use a serrated-edged knife to cut the skin and pith from the oranges in a sawing motion. Then cut down between the membranes to make orange segments. Mix the melon balls and orange segments in each melon half and sprinkle them all very lightly with sugar.

Cover each melon half with plastic wrap until ready to serve.

Cookie Press Shortbread

$2\frac{1}{4}$ cups flour
pinch of salt
$\frac{1}{2}$ teaspoon baking powder
1 cup butter, at room temperature
$\frac{3}{4}$ cup sugar
1 egg
1 teaspoon vanilla

Cookie press for forming 'S' shapes

Method

Set the oven at 375°F. Sift the flour, salt and baking powder. Cream the butter until soft and light. Add the sugar gradually and beat well. Add the egg and vanilla, then stir in the flour. Form double S-shaped cookies with a cookie press, putting them onto an ungreased baking sheet. Bake for 12–15 minutes or until set but not browned.

Easter Cookies

2 cups flour
pinch of salt
$\frac{2}{3}$ cup (almost 11 tablespoons) butter, at room temperature
grated rind of 1 lemon
$\frac{2}{3}$ cup sugar
2 egg yolks
$\frac{1}{2}$ cup currants
1 egg white, lightly beaten (for glaze)
sugar (for sprinkling)

$3\frac{1}{2}$-inch fluted cutter

This quantity makes 22–24 cookies.

Method

Set the oven at 375°F. Very lightly grease a baking sheet.

Sift the flour with the salt. Cream the butter until soft and light, beat in the lemon rind and sugar and continue beating until the mixture is no longer granular. Add the yolks, one at a time, followed by the sifted flour and currants. Knead lightly on a floured board until smooth; then wrap it in plastic film and refrigerate for 1 hour.

Roll out the mixture between two sheets of waxed paper and use the cutter to stamp out rounds. Brush with egg white, sprinkle with sugar and bake on the prepared baking sheet for 12–15 minutes, or until just lightly browned. Collect the trimmings, reroll them in waxed paper then stamp, glaze and bake as before.

Brioches Mousseline

2 cups flour
1 envelope dried yeast or
1 cake compressed yeast
about 2 tablespoons lukewarm milk
2 eggs
2 tablespoons sugar
pinch of salt
$\frac{1}{2}$ cup butter, at room temperature
grated rind of $\frac{1}{2}$ lemon
$\frac{1}{2}$ cup golden raisins
2 tablespoons glacé cherries, halved
2 tablespoons candied peel, chopped
1 egg, beaten to mix (for glaze)

6-inch diameter brioche mold

Method

Mix the yeast with $\frac{1}{2}$ cup of the flour and the milk to form a dough. Cut a cross on top and set the dough in a bowl of warm water. Leave for 10 minutes.

Mix the remaining flour with the eggs, sugar and salt until very elastic. Add the butter and drained ball of yeast. Stir well to mix and cover with plastic film. Refrigerate overnight.

Turn the dough out onto a lightly floured board and work in the lemon rind, raisins, cherries and candied peel. Shape the dough into a neat round and pinch off a piece the size of an egg. Butter the brioche mold and set the large piece of dough in it. Cut a small cross in the top of the dough. Shape the smaller piece into a neat ball and set it right on the cross. Brush the top with the egg glaze and leave to rise for 1 hour or until the dough has reached the top of the pans.

Preheat the oven to 450°F. Bake the brioche for 45 minutes or until firm to the touch and golden brown. Turn out onto a rack and leave until cool.

Spiced Rolls

1 recipe Brioche Mousseline (left to rise overnight without fruits)
3 tablespoons butter, melted

For filling
2 tablespoons butter, at room temperature
$\frac{1}{4}$ cup dark brown sugar
$\frac{1}{4}$ teaspoon cinnamon
$\frac{1}{8}$ teaspoon ginger
$\frac{1}{2}$ cup chopped walnuts or almonds

For topping
$\frac{1}{4}$ cup butter
$\frac{1}{4}$ cup dark brown sugar
$\frac{1}{2}$ cup broken walnuts

Deep 12-cup muffin pan

Method

Turn the cold dough out onto a lightly floured board and roll it, flouring the pin as necessary to prevent the dough from sticking, to a $\frac{1}{2}$-inch thick oblong about 12 by 9 inches. Use the 3 tablespoons melted butter to butter the muffin cups.

For the filling: mix together the soft butter, brown sugar, cinnamon, ginger and walnuts. Spread this on the oblong of dough and roll it up jelly-roll fashion. Set aside for a minute.

For the topping: melt the $\frac{1}{4}$ cup butter with the dark brown sugar and, when dissolved, stir in the broken walnuts. Divide this mixture evenly among the greased muffin cups.

Cut the roll of dough into 12 even slices and set one in each cup. Leave to rise for 15 minutes.

Preheat the oven to 375°F. Bake the rolls on the top shelf of the hot oven for 18–20 minutes or until firm to the touch.

Turn the hot muffin pan upside down onto a baking sheet, leave for several minutes, then carefully lift off the pan. Cool for 15 minutes, and serve hot, or cool completely for serving.

Heckles

$\frac{1}{3}$ cup sugar
3 tablespoons water
2 cups flour
$\frac{1}{2}$ cup butter, cut up

This quantity yields 19 cookies.

Method

Put the sugar and water into a small saucepan and bring them slowly to the boil, stirring with a spoon once or twice so the sugar dissolves before the water boils. Take the pan from the heat and leave it to cool completely.

Sift the flour into a bowl and cut in the butter until the mixture resembles breadcrumbs. Rub the butter in with your fingers to aerate the dough. Set the oven at 375°F.

Scrape the sugar syrup from the saucepan with a rubber spatula and stir it into the dough with a blunt knife until all the dry ingredients are wet. Then turn the dough onto a lightly floured board and knead very gently until smooth.

Divide the dough into 19 even pieces. Keep the pieces covered with a cloth while you roll one out with a lightly floured pin until it is about $3\frac{1}{2}$-inches across. The edges will be very raggedy. Transfer the heckle to an ungreased sheet and prick it a dozen times in the center with a fork.

Continue rolling and pricking the heckles until they are all on the baking sheet. Bake them in the preheated oven for 10 minutes or until the edges are just beginning to brown. Lift at once onto a wire rack to cool.

The cakes and cookies given here are many more than you will need for your brunch guests, but we offer them as alternatives and so you will have a selection to choose from on those days when you feel like baking for the freezer.

Hot Blueberry Quick Bread

$\frac{1}{4}$ cup butter, at room temperature
1 cup sugar
1 egg
1 teaspoon vanilla extract
$1\frac{2}{3}$ cups flour
$\frac{1}{2}$ teaspoon salt
1 teaspoon baking powder
1 cup milk
$1\frac{1}{2}$ cups fresh blueberries, washed and picked over
$\frac{1}{4}$ cup flour (for dusting blueberries)
granulated sugar (for sprinkling)

Two $7\frac{1}{2}$ x $3\frac{1}{2}$ x $2\frac{1}{2}$-inch loaf pans

Method

Grease the loaf pans, line them with waxed paper so it comes an inch above the sides of the pans and grease the paper also. Dust it with sugar, tapping out the excess.

Set the oven at 350°F.

Cream the butter, gradually add the sugar and keep beating until it is all incorporated. The mixture will look very dry at this point.

Add the egg and vanilla and beat to mix.

Sift the $1\frac{2}{3}$ cup of flour with the salt and baking powder. Add the dry ingredients to the batter alternately with the milk, beginning and ending with flour.

Spoon enough batter into both pans to make a thin layer on the bottom. Set aside. Combine the blueberries (which should be wet from washing) with the $\frac{1}{4}$ cup flour and stir with a rubber spatula until all are coated. Now stir blueberries into the remaining batter with the spatula until they are distributed. Divide the batter between the pans and sprinkle loaves with the sugar. Bake them in the preheated oven for 65 minutes or until the tops are golden brown and the breads are firm. Turn them out of the pans and leave to cool for 15 minutes. Then peel away the paper and cool completely; or peel away the paper and serve at once.

Hungarian Coffee Cake

$3\frac{1}{2}$ cups flour
1 teaspoon salt
1 cup milk, scalded and cooled to lukewarm
$\frac{1}{4}$ cup sugar
1 envelope dried yeast or 1 cake compressed yeast
$\frac{1}{4}$ cup butter, melted and cooled to lukewarm
1 egg, beaten to mix

For filling
$\frac{1}{2}$ cup butter
1 cup sugar
1 teaspoon cinnamon
$\frac{1}{2}$ cup almond slivers, finely chopped
$\frac{1}{2}$ cup raisins

9-inch diameter tube pan

Method

Sift the flour and salt into a bowl. Pour in the lukewarm milk, add the sugar, sprinkle in the dried yeast or crumble in the compressed yeast and leave for 5 minutes.

Add the butter and egg to the flour and stir well with a wooden spoon to form a dough. Turn out onto a lightly floured board and knead until smooth. Put the dough into a greased bowl, turn it over so the other side is greased also, and cover with a damp cloth.

Leave the dough to rise in a warm place for 45 minutes or until doubled in bulk.

Punch down the dough and recover with the damp cloth. Leave it to rise again for 30 minutes.

Turn the dough out onto a lightly floured board and divide it into about 24 walnut sized pieces. Cover and let them rest for 10 minutes.

Thoroughly grease the tube pan.

For the filling: melt the butter and put it on a plate.

Mix the sugar, cinnamon, and chopped almonds on a plate.

Shape each piece of dough into a ball and roll each one first in the melted butter, then into the sugar-almond mixture. Put a layer of half the balls in the bottom of the tube pan. Sprinkle with the raisins. Make another layer with the remaining balls. Cover the pan with a damp cloth and leave to rise for 1 hour or until the cake has doubled in bulk.

Meanwhile, set the oven at 375°F. When the oven is hot, bake the coffee cake for 45 minutes or until very brown and firm to the touch. Loosen the cake from the sides of the pan with a long metal palette knife, then turn the cake out onto a round platter and leave until still warm. Serve with two forks, breaking the cake apart into clusters of the balls for each serving.

Rich Currant Bread

$2\frac{1}{2}$ cups flour
pinch of salt
1 tablespoon sugar
1 envelope dried yeast or 1 cake compressed yeast
$\frac{1}{2}$ cup milk
1 egg, beaten to mix
4 tablespoons butter, at room temperature
large pinch saffron threads (soaked for 1 hour in 2 tablespoons hot water)
$\frac{3}{4}$ cup currants
2 tablespoons milk mixed with 1 tablespoon sugar (for glaze)

$8\frac{1}{2}$ x $4\frac{1}{2}$ x $2\frac{1}{2}$-inch loaf pan

Method
Sift the flour with the salt into a large bowl. Stir the sugar and yeast together. Warm the milk just to lukewarm and add to the yeast mixture with the egg and butter. Stir these liquids into the flour with the saffron liquid.

Mix well and knead lightly on a floured board to form a smooth dough. Cover with a damp cloth and leave in a warm place to rise for 45 minutes to 1 hour.

Punch down the dough and work in the currants. Butter the loaf pan and form the dough into a neat rectangular shape. Put it into the pan, seam side down, and leave to rise for 1 hour, or until dough is right to the top of the pan.

Preheat the oven to 400°F. Bake the bread for 35–40 minutes or until golden brown. Five minutes before the end of baking, brush the top of the bread with the sweetened milk and return to the oven to finish cooking.

Turn out onto a rack to cool.

Ischel

$\frac{3}{4}$ cup butter, at room temperature
$\frac{1}{4}$ cup sugar
1 cup ground almonds
$1\frac{1}{2}$ cups flour

For the chocolate glacé icing
3 squares (3 oz) semisweet chocolate
3 tablespoons water
$1\frac{1}{2}$ cups confectioners' sugar
3 tablespoons sugar syrup or water

To finish
3 tablespoons apricot jam
2 squares (2 oz) unsweetened chocolate

2-inch round cutter; parchment paper

This quantity yields 26 sandwiched cookies.

Method
Set the oven at 350°F. Grease and flour a baking sheet.

Cream the butter, beat in the sugar gradually, then work in the ground almonds and flour to form a dough. Knead lightly on a floured board, then wrap in plastic film and chill 15 minutes.

Roll the dough to an eighth-inch thick round and stamp out rounds with the cutter. Place them on the baking sheet and bake in the preheated oven for 8–10 minutes or until straw-colored.

Lift the cookies onto a rack to cool. Sandwich the rounds with the apricot jam and set them on a cake rack with a large sheet of waxed paper underneath.

For the chocolate glacé icing: melt the chocolate in the water over a gentle heat, stirring until it is smooth. Take from the heat and beat in the confectioners' sugar. Add enough of the sugar syrup or water to make a thick cream, then stir the saucepan over a bowl of hot water until it is just warm to the touch and coats the back of a spoon. If it is too thick, add a few more drops of the water. If it is too thin, beat in a few more tablespoons of confectioners' sugar.

With a small ladle, pour the icing over the cookies and leave them for 20 minutes or until set.

Melt the unsweetened chocolate on a plate over a pan of hot water, working it well with a metal palette knife until smooth.

Make a piping bag from the parchment paper, fill it with the chocolate and cut the smallest possible tip from the pointed end. Pipe lines to form a lattice on each cookie and leave them for 30 minutes or until completely set.

Souvaroffs

1 cup flour
pinch of salt
$\frac{1}{4}$ cup sugar
7 tablespoons butter, at room temperature
confectioners' sugar (for sprinkling)
$\frac{1}{4}$ cup red currant jelly

2-inch oval or round fluted cutter

Makes 12 sandwiched cookies.

Method
Sift the flour with the salt onto a pastry board. Make a well in the center and add the sugar and butter. Work the sugar and butter together and gradually work in the flour to make a dough. Knead the dough until smooth, wrap in plastic film and refrigerate for one hour.

Roll out the dough between two sheets of waxed paper and stamp out oval or round shapes. Transfer them to a baking sheet and refrigerate 15 minutes. Set the oven at 400°F.

Bake the cookies in the preheated oven for 8 minutes. Take them from the oven and turn on the broiler. Dredge the tops of half the cookies with confectioners' sugar and slide under the broiler for 10 seconds, or until the sugar caramelizes.

Take from the oven and leave until cool. When cold, sandwich the cookies with the red currant jelly, spreading it on the plain cookies and topping them with the glazed ones.

Left: Lamb and rosemary hotpot with fried spinach; right: Baked apples with orange and raisins

INFORMAL SATURDAY SUPPER FOR 4

Lamb and Rosemary Hotpot

Fried Spinach

Orange and Raisin Stuffed Apples

*Red wine – Châteauneuf du Pape (Rhône)
or Zinfandel (California)*

We tend to use Saturdays as a day to get errands done and when we want to have supper with friends on that weekend night, there never seems to be enough time to do everything in one short day. The menu that follows will allow you to do chores around the house while the main course cooks and you'll be able to do the spinach accompaniment at the last minute.

Ginger-flavored baked apples finish this informal meal (or choose one of the other kinds we offer on these pages), and you'll find you've had plenty of time to do the gardening you meant to do all week – and sit down and relax during the evening. A carafe of red wine would be the perfect accompaniment to this meal at the end of a busy day.

Entrée

Lamb and Rosemary Hotpot

12 lamb loin chops
2 medium onions, sliced
2 medium carrots, sliced and blanched 3 minutes
1 teaspoon dried rosemary
salt and pepper
2 lb potatoes, peeled and left in cold water
1 tablespoon red currant jelly
1 cup chicken stock
2 tablespoons oil

Method
Preheat the oven to 350°F. Put 6 lamb chops in the bottom of a casserole. Scatter half the onion, carrot and rosemary on top. Sprinkle with salt and pepper and repeat the layers with the remaining lamb and vegetables.

Thinly slice the potatoes and arrange them on top of the vegetables in overlapping concentric circles. Heat the red currant jelly with the stock and pour it into the casserole. Spoon the oil on top of the potatoes and sprinkle with salt and pepper.

Cover the casserole and bake it in the preheated oven for $1\frac{1}{2}$ hours, or until the potatoes and meat are both tender when tested with a skewer from the top of the casserole. Uncover the pan and continue cooking for another 20 minutes or until the potatoes are lightly browned. Serve with fried spinach.

Accompaniment to entrée

Fried Spinach

3 tablespoons oil
1 small onion, finely chopped
1 clove of garlic, crushed
2 lb fresh spinach, washed with stalks removed
juice of $\frac{1}{2}$ lemon
salt and pepper

Method
Heat the oil in a large kettle and fry the onion gently until soft but not brown. Add the garlic and continue cooking another minute.

Meanwhile, tear the large spinach leaves in half. Add the spinach to the pan with the lemon juice and continue cooking over a gentle heat, stirring constantly, until the spinach wilts and is just tender. Add plenty of salt and pepper, stir well and serve.

Dessert

Orange and Raisin Stuffed Apples

4 medium cooking apples
1 cup raisins
$\frac{1}{4}$ cup dark brown sugar
$\frac{1}{2}$ teaspoon ginger
1 large juice orange

Method
Set the oven at 350°F. Use an apple corer to core the fruits. Make a very shallow horizontal cut around the apples to prevent the skins from bursting while they cook. Put the apples in a buttered ovenproof dish.

Mix the raisins, dark brown sugar and ginger together. Grate the rind from the orange and mix it into the raisins. Press some of the filling in each hollowed apple core, spooning any excess into the dish.

Squeeze the juice from the orange and pour it over and around the apples. Bake them in the preheated oven for 45 minutes or until the apples are tender.

Serve hot or cold with the juices from the dish spooned over them.

Alternative desserts

Spicy Date Stuffed Apples

Core 4 apples and slit the skins horizontally. Chop $\frac{1}{4}$ cup pitted dates and mix with grated rind and juice of 1 orange, $\frac{1}{2}$ teaspoon cinnamon, pinch ground cloves and 2 tablespoons dark brown sugar. Fill cavities, set in a buttered ovenproof dish and bake as above.

Cherry Baked Apples

Core 4 apples and slit skins horizontally. Mix half a can of cherry pie filling with 1 teaspoon grated orange rind and 1 tablespoon brandy. Fill cavities with cherry filling and bake as above. Serve with unwhipped unsweetened heavy cream.

Hawaiian Baked Apples

Core 4 apples and slit skins horizontally. Peel apples down to slit. Beat 4 tablespoons soft butter with 4 tablespoons sugar. Chop 2 pineapple slices and add to apple cavities. Top with some of the butter-sugar mixture, spreading it on the peeled portion. Bake in a buttered ovenproof dish, as above, then scatter tops with coconut. Heat 2 tablespoons butter in a skillet and fry 4 pineapple slices quickly on both sides. Place a slice of pineapple on each apple and serve.

Marshmallow and Cranberry Stuffed Apples

Spread a buttered ovenproof dish with half a can of cranberry sauce. Add 2 tablespoons water. Core and slit 4 apples as in previous recipes, then peel them down to slits around center. Put apples, peeled side down into cranberry mixture. Bake apples for 15 minutes.

Turn them right side up. Coarsely chop 2 tablespoons walnuts and mix with $\frac{1}{2}$ cup chopped marshmallow pieces. Press this mixture into the apple cavities and put a spoonful of the sauce from the bottom of the dish into each one. Return to the oven and continue baking another 30 minutes.

Zabaglione Apples

Core and slit 4 apples as in previous recipes and bake them in a buttered shallow ovenproof dish for 45 minutes as above. Leave to cool completely.

Put 3 egg yolks and 3 tablespoons sugar with 1 teaspoon grated lemon rind in a saucepan over another pan filled with hot, but not boiling, water. Whisk the yolks steadily for 1 minute, then gradually whisk in $\frac{1}{2}$ cup Marsala. Continue whisking until the mixture doubles in volume and is very thick and mousse-like. Pour this mixture over the apples and sprinkle them with some chopped pistachio nuts.

Mincemeat Apple Cups

Core 4 apples and hollow out flesh so you are left with inch-thick shells. Chop the flesh and put it into a bowl with $\frac{1}{4}$ cup mincemeat and 1 tablespoon dark brown sugar. Fill apples with the mincemeat mixture and set in a buttered baking dish. Pour in 3 tablespoons water and 3 tablespoons orange juice. Sprinkle apples with dark brown sugar and bake for 45 minutes.

Almond Meringue Apples

Core and slit 4 apples as in previous recipes. Peel them down to the center slits. Mix $\frac{1}{4}$ cup chopped almonds with $\frac{1}{4}$ cup sugar. Place apples in a buttered shallow ovenproof dish and fill centers with almond mixture. Bake for 45 minutes. Beat 1 egg white until stiff and beat in 2 tablespoons sugar. Fold in another 1 tablespoon sugar with 1 tablespoon fresh white breadcrumbs. Pour this mixture over the apples and sprinkle with more breadcrumbs. Bake in a 400°F oven for a few minutes or until browned.

More baked apples from which to choose: Marshmallow and cranberry (left), Almond meringue apples (right) – just two out of a mouthwatering selection

This Coffee meringue gâteau just melts in the mouth. It is flavored with nuts and cinnamon, decorated with whipped cream and hazelnuts and served with a rich, dark coffee sauce flavored with rum

A CLASSIC FRENCH COUNTRY DINNER

Potage Crème Créole

Casserole de Poulet Brabançonne
Purée of Carrots with Parmesan

Coffee Meringue Gâteau with Sauce Moka
or
Chocolate and Chestnut Profiteroles

White wine – Pouilly Fumé (Loire)
or Fumé Blanc (California)

Begin this elegant dinner with a creamy rose-colored soup made with a purée of pimientos and tomatoes, spiced with cayenne and horseradish. The chicken entrée has been cooked with lean salt pork and plenty of onions in ale and is topped with crusty French bread. The cake for dessert – made from rounds of nut-flavored meringue and sandwiched with a coffee cream – is very professionally decorated. Or, fill cream puffs with a chestnut cream and pass them with chocolate sauce spooned on top.

Our wine consultant suggests you serve a chilled white wine, a flinty Pouilly Fumé from the Loire region of France, or its Californian counterpart, Fumé Blanc, with the chicken casserole.

TIMETABLE

Day before

Prepare the soup and purée it *(if not already in freezer)* but do not add spices or seasonings.
Make the rounds for the meringue cake *or make the cream puffs*; store the rounds in an airtight container, *the cream puffs in a bowl, loosely covered.*

Cook the carrots and purée them; store in a covered container in refrigerator.
Remove chicken dish from freezer (and soup if frozen in advance).

Morning of party

Make moka sauce *or filling for cream puffs and chocolate sauce.*
Assemble meringue cake and decorate or assemble cream puffs.
Prepare chicken without putting rolls on top.

Order of work

7:00
Set the oven at 350°F.

7:20
Reheat chocolate sauce, if using, over a double boiler. Put the chicken in the oven to reheat.

7:40
Reheat carrot purée with cream and keep in a water bath. Put French bread slices on top of chicken and continue cooking.

7:50
Reheat soup; keep warm.

8:00
Swirl cream into soup and serve. After the first course plates have been cleared, add cheese to carrots

> Cooking times in individual recipes have sometimes been adjusted to help you when cooking and serving this menu as a three-course meal.

These raw ingredients are combined and transformed into Potage crème créole (at right)

The finished soup is swirled with cream before serving. It is flavored with pimiento and tomato and spiked with horseradish. This soup, like many others in this volume, can be frozen

Appetizer

Potage Crème Créole

1 small onion, finely chopped
2 tablespoons butter
$\frac{1}{4}$ cup shredded canned pimiento
3 tablespoons flour
1 can (1 lb) Italian-style plum tomatoes
5 cups well-flavored chicken stock
salt and pepper
pinch cayenne pepper
1 teaspoon prepared horseradish
$\frac{1}{4}$ cup heavy cream (to finish)

Method

Cook the onion in the butter in a saucepan until soft but not brown. Add the pimiento and stir in the flour. Crush the tomatoes one at a time in your hand as you add them to the pan. Pour in the stock with plenty of salt and pepper to taste and bring to a boil.

Cover and simmer the soup for 25 minutes or until the tomatoes are very pulpy. Work the soup through a food mill into a clean saucepan and stir in the cayenne and horseradish. Taste for seasoning and return just to the boil.

Pour the soup into a warm tureen, add the cream with one hand as you swirl it into the top with the tip of a spoon held in the other hand. Serve at once.

To freeze Allow to cool and pack in cartons for freezing as soon as the horseradish has been added.

Thawing and serving Leave overnight in the refrigerator before pouring into a pan to reheat. Bring the soup to the boil and continue as recipe.

Entreé

Casserole de Poulet Brabançonne

$\frac{1}{2}$ lb roasting chicken
$\frac{1}{2}$ lb lean salt pork
2 tablespoons oil
2 tablespoons butter
4 medium onions, sliced
salt and pepper
$1\frac{1}{2}$ cups ale
1 cup chicken stock
1 teaspoon sugar
2 small French breads
2 tablespoons soft butter (for the rolls)
1 tablespoon Dijon-style mustard

Method
Remove the giblets and pockets of fat from the bird and set the oven at 325°F.

Put the salt pork into a saucepan with water to cover. Bring to a boil and simmer for 30 minutes, then drain; set aside.

Heat the oil in a deep flameproof casserole. Add the butter and when foaming, lower the heat and brown the bird slowly on all sides. Meanwhile, remove any rind from the salt pork and cut it into strips. Take the chicken from the casserole and put in the salt pork and onions and cook gently until both are browned. Take the pan from the heat and lift out the onions and salt pork with a slotted spoon.

Cut the chicken into 8 pieces, using poultry shears and a heavy knife. Remove the fat from the casserole and replace the chicken in it with the onions and pork. Add plenty of freshly ground black pepper to taste and pour in the ale with half the stock. Add the sugar and bring to a boil. Cover and put in the oven. Cook for 15 minutes.

Meanwhile, slice the French breads. Mix the soft butter with the mustard and spread this on the bread. Arrange the croûtes on the top of the casserole and spoon over the remaining stock. Return to the oven, uncovered, and increase the heat to 375°F. Cook the casserole for 30 minutes or until the top is browned and crisp.

Serve with carrot purée.

To freeze Pack and freeze after allowing the casserole to cool.

Thawing and serving Thaw in the refrigerator for 24 hours, then reheat, uncovered, in a moderate oven, 350°F, for 35–40 minutes until boiling.

Accompaniment to entrée

Purée of Carrots with Parmesan

1 lb carrots, thinly sliced
$\frac{1}{2}$ small onion, grated
2 tablespoons butter
2 tablespoons flour
1 cup heavy cream
salt and pepper
pinch of grated nutmeg
$\frac{1}{3}$ cup freshly grated Parmesan cheese

Method
Put the carrots on the rack of a vegetable steamer and insert the steamer into a deep saucepan. Add several inches of water and cover the pan. Bring to a boil and steam for 20 minutes or until the carrots are very tender. Drain them and work them through the fine blade of a food mill into a bowl. Stir in the grated onion.

Melt the butter in a saucepan and stir in the flour. Cook for two minutes or until the roux begins to turn a pale straw color and whisk in the cream, stirring constantly. Simmer a couple of minutes, then add the salt and pepper and nutmeg and whisk in the carrot purée a little at a time. Bring the mixture just back to the boil and taste for seasoning.

Keep warm in a water bath, if necessary, and stir in the Parmesan cheese just before serving.

For Casserole de poulet brabançonne, the chicken is browned and cooked in ale with salt pork and onions. The top is covered with slices of French bread spread with mustard, and the whole dish is finished in the oven until the topping is crisp

A French country dinner

Pipe rosettes of cream on top of the meringue cake after the cream-filled rounds have thawed. Use a star tip and keep the bag in an upright position while piping the rosettes

Dessert

Coffee Meringue Gâteau

4 egg whites
1 1/4 cups granulated sugar
1/2 teaspoon cinnamon
3/4 cup ground hazelnuts

For filling
1 1/2 teaspoons dry instant coffee
2 tablespoons dark brown sugar
2 tablespoons hot water
1 cup heavy cream

For decoration
confectioners' sugar (for sprinkling)
1/2 cup heavy cream, stiffly whipped
coffee bean candies or whole hazelnuts (for decorating)

2 baking sheets lined with parchment paper; pastry bag; 3/8-inch plain round and star tips

Method

Set the oven at 250°F.

Beat the egg whites until stiff, add 1 tablespoon of the measured granulated sugar and continue beating for 30 seconds or until they are glossy.

Sift the remaining sugar with the cinnamon and fold it into the whites with the ground hazelnuts. Pile the meringue mixture into a pastry bag fitted with the plain round tip and pipe two 8-inch rounds on the baking sheets lined with parchment paper. Bake the meringues in the preheated oven for 1–1 1/4 hours or until firm to the touch. Leave the rounds to cool completely.

Mix the instant coffee with the brown sugar and hot water and leave until completely cool. Whip the 1 cup heavy cream until it holds a soft shape. Add the coffee syrup and continue beating until the mixture is stiff. Sandwich the cooled meringue rounds with the coffee cream, setting the top round right side up.

To freeze Wrap in foil and freeze.

Thawing and serving Allow to thaw at room temperature for 4 hours.

Dust the top with confectioners' sugar. Fill the stiffly whipped cream into a pastry bag fitted with a star tip and pipe rosettes around the top edge of the cake. Stud these with the coffee bean candies or hazelnuts and refrigerate until serving.

Sauce Moka

1 1/3 cups sugar
1 1/2 cups water
1 tablespoon dry instant coffee dissolved in 1 tablespoon warm water
1 tablespoon rum
1/2 cup heavy cream

Method

Put the sugar and half the water into a heavy-based saucepan and dissolve it over very low heat. Then bring to a boil and boil steadily until the mixture is a dark brown caramel color. Take the pan from the heat and add the remaining water.

Watchpoint Hold a cloth over your hand as you add the water; the caramel will splutter quite a bit as the cold water touches the hot sugar mixture.

Cook the caramel over a gentle heat until dissolved. Leave to cool slightly, then stir in the dissolved coffee and rum and leave until cold.

Stir in the heavy cream and pour into a sauceboat.

Alternative dessert

Chocolate and Chestnut Profiteroles

For choux puffs
2/3 cup flour
1/4 teaspoon salt
2/3 cup water
1/3 cup butter, cut up
3–4 eggs

For filling
1 cup heavy cream
1 can (8 oz) sweetened chestnut purée

For chocolate sauce
8 squares (8 oz) semi-sweet chocolate
3/4 cup water
1/2 cup sugar
1/4 cup heavy cream

Pastry bag and 1/4-inch plain round tip

This quantity makes 3 dozen cream puffs.

Method

For the choux puffs: sift the flour and salt onto a sheet of waxed paper. Put the water and butter into a fairly large saucepan and bring slowly to the boil so the butter melts before the liquid is bubbling. Let the mixture boil vigorously for one second, then take the pan from the heat and shoot in the flour all at once. Beat for a few seconds until the mixture is smooth and forms a ball in the bottom of the pan, then stir it over a low heat for 30 seconds to dry it out. Turn out onto a plate to cool for 5 minutes.

Set the oven at 400°F and very lightly grease a baking sheet, then dampen it with drops of tap water sprinkled on with your hand.

Return the mixture to the saucepan and beat in the eggs one at a time, beating well after each addition. Beat the last egg in a small bowl and add it to the mixture a few drops at a time. The choux paste should just drop from a spoon, but still hold its shape. All of the last egg might not be needed.

Beat the dough for two minutes or until it is glossy, then pile it into the pastry bag fitted with the plain round tip and pipe mounds of the mixture far apart on the dampened baking sheet.

Bake them for 10 minutes, then raise the temperature and continue baking for 10–15 minutes or until the puffs are very firm to the touch. Take from the oven, prick on one side with the tip of a knife so the steam escapes, and cool on a wire rack.

For the filling: whip the cream until it holds a soft shape; stir the chestnut purée to soften it, then fold in the whipped cream.

Fill the pastry bag fitted with the plain round tip with the cream and pipe the mixture into each puff. Mound the puffs on a large platter and refrigerate.

For the chocolate sauce: put the chocolate and water and sugar in a saucepan and stir them over a low heat until the chocolate melts and the mixture is smooth. Take from the heat and stir in the heavy cream. Leave in a water bath until ready to serve the profiteroles with the sauce spooned over them.

An unusual variation on a theme, a hot fruit salad made from dried fruits flavored with sherry and cinnamon

FRUIT PUDDINGS AND DESSERTS

After a rich or filling entrée, the only real refreshing way to end the meal is with fresh fruit, or a fruit pudding or a cooling fruit dessert. Here we offer you interesting ways with peaches, dried fruits, cherries, plums, lemons, apricots, strawberries, bananas, apricots, and several other fruits.

HOT DESSERTS

Hot Fruit Salad

$\frac{1}{4}$ cup pitted prunes
$\frac{1}{4}$ cup dried apricots
$\frac{1}{4}$ cup dried pears
$\frac{1}{4}$ cup dried apple rings
2 tablespoons raisins
2 sticks of cinnamon
2 cups dry white wine and water, mixed
$\frac{1}{2}$ cup light brown sugar
2 tablespoons dry sherry
1 cup heavy cream mixed with $\frac{1}{4}$ teaspoon ground cinnamon (for serving)

Method
Put the prunes, apricots, pears, apples, raisins, cinnamon and white wine and water into a large bowl. Turn well, cover with plastic wrap and refrigerate overnight.

Set the oven at 350°F. Transfer the fruits and the juice to a casserole, add the sugar and cover. Set in the preheated oven and bake for 30–40 minutes or until the mixture is very hot. Stir in the sherry and serve with crisp cookies and the flavored heavy cream.

Baked Lemon Pudding

4 tablespoons butter
grated rind and juice of 1 lemon
$\frac{2}{3}$ cup sugar
2 eggs, separated
$1\frac{1}{2}$ tablespoons flour
1 cup milk

Soufflé dish (1 quart capacity)

Method
Set the oven at 350°F. Thoroughly grease the soufflé dish.

Beat the butter until soft and light. Add the grated lemon rind and gradually add the sugar, beating constantly until it is very light and fluffy. Meanwhile, bring a tea kettle of water to the boil.

Beat in the yolks, one at a time, followed by the flour. Add the lemon juice and milk and beat just to mix.

Whisk the egg whites until they form stiff peaks and fold them into the lemon mixture with a large metal spoon. Turn the batter into the dish and set it in a roasting pan; put the roasting pan in the oven, pull out the rack, and pour the boiling water around the soufflé dish so it comes halfway up the sides. Slip the rack into the oven and bake the pudding for 45–50 minutes or until the pudding is just set. Serve at once. The mixture separates during cooking and will look something like a honeycomb when apportioned.

Cherry Pudding

$1\frac{1}{2}$ lb fresh Bing or Royal Anne cherries, pitted
$\frac{3}{4}$ cup sugar
1 cup water
2 tablespoons cornstarch mixed with 3 tablespoons water
2 teaspoons lemon juice
3 tablespoon butter, at room temperature
5–6 slices white bread, crusts removed
granulated sugar (for sprinkling)

Method
Set the oven at 350°F. Lightly grease a shallow baking dish. Combine the cherries, sugar and water in a saucepan and bring slowly to a boil, stirring occasionally, until the sugar has dissolved. Simmer gently for 5 minutes or until the cherries are just tender. Add the cornstarch paste to the cherry mixture and return to the boil. Add the lemon juice and cook 1 minute. Taste this mixture for seasoning and add more sugar or lemon juice according to your taste.

Pour the cherry mixture into the shallow dish. Use the soft butter to butter one side of the bread and cut them into triangles. Sprinkle the buttered side with some granulated sugar and arrange the triangles on the cherries in overlapping rows.

Bake the pudding in the preheated oven for 20 minutes, or until the bread is just beginning to brown at the edges and the cherry pudding is bubbling at the sides. Serve at once with a pitcher of heavy cream.

Plum Crumble

2 lb plums
3 cups cake crumbs (from a white cake, pound cake or any other firm-textured cake)
$\frac{1}{4}$ cup ground almonds
$\frac{1}{2}$ teaspoon ground cinnamon
grated rind of 1 lemon
$\frac{3}{4}$ cup light corn syrup
2 tablespoons butter, melted
3 tablespoons sliced almonds

Method
Halve the plums, remove the pits and cut each half in half again.

Set the oven at 400°F and lightly grease a small deep baking dish.

Put cake crumbs, ground almonds, cinnamon and lemon rind in a bowl and stir to mix. Put a layer of the dry ingredients in the baking dish and cover with a layer of plums. Dribble over some of the syrup and continue layering until the crumbs, fruit and golden syrup are all used, ending with a layer of crumbs.

Spoon the melted butter on top and sprinkle with the almonds. Bake in the preheated oven for 30 minutes or until the plums are tender when pierced with a skewer.

New ways with fruit

Plum crumble, sprinkled with almonds, will soon become a favorite family dessert

Raspberry Custard Crème

2 packages frozen raspberries thawed, or 2 pints fresh raspberries
1 egg, separated
1 egg yolk
1 tablespoon sugar
½ teaspoon vanilla
2 tablespoons flour
1 tablespoon cornstarch
1¼ cups milk
½ cup heavy cream, stiffly whipped
1 tablespoon finely chopped pistachio nuts

Pastry bag and star tip

Method

Open the packages of frozen raspberries and drain them (reserve the juice for another use). Or halve the fresh raspberries, reserving 4 perfect ones.

Beat the 2 egg yolks, sugar and vanilla together. Stir in the flour and cornstarch. Add enough of the milk to make a smooth paste. Scald the remaining milk and when it is very hot, pour it onto the yolk mixture, whisking constantly. Then return the entire mixture to the saucepan and bring to a boil, stirring, until it thickens. Lower the heat and simmer 2 minutes, still stirring. Leave to cool.

Beat the egg white until it holds stiff peaks and fold it into the warm mixture. Fold in the frozen or fresh raspberries and put the mixture into four individual coupe glasses or stemmed glasses.

Refrigerate for several hours or until completely cold. Fill the whipped cream into the pastry bag and pipe a rosette of cream on each serving. Top with a fresh raspberry (if using) and sprinkle the cream with the chopped pistachios. Return to the refrigerator until ready to serve.

Banana Almond Bake

8 almond macaroons
4 large firm bananas
¾ cup heavy cream
1 jar (1 lb) unsweetened applesauce
½ teaspoon vanilla extract
¼ cup sugar
2 tablespoon lemon juice
2 tablespoon red currant jelly

Method

Set the oven at 400°F and grease a 5-cup baking dish. Crush the macaroons and set half in the bottom of the dish.

Whip the cream until it holds soft peaks and fold it into the applesauce with the vanilla and sugar. Put this into the dish and level the surface with a spatula.

Peel the bananas and cut them on the diagonal into slices. Sprinkle with lemon juice. Arrange the banana slices overlapping on the apple mixture.

Heat the red currant jelly in a small saucepan until melted. Pour it over the bananas. Cover with the remaining macaroons. Bake the bananas in the preheated oven for 15 minutes or until bubbling at the edges and golden brown on top.

Baked Pineapple Crisp

1 medium pineapple, peeled and sliced
1 tablespoon sugar
2 tablespoons water
grated rind and juice of 1 lemon
⅔ cup rolled oats
4 tablespoons butter, melted
¼ cup chopped mixed nuts (walnuts, almonds, pecans), browned
¼ teaspoon ground cinnamon

Method

Core the pineapple slices and put them in the bottom of a buttered shallow ovenproof dish. Set the oven at 375°F.

Sprinkle the sugar over the pineapple and pour in the water, lemon rind and juice.

Put the rolled oats in a bowl and pour in the melted butter, nuts and ground cinnamon. Spread this over the pineapple slices and bake the dish in the preheated oven for 30 minutes or until the top is browned and crisp. Serve at once.

Rhubarb and Pecan Crumble

1½ lb rhubarb, trimmed
¾ cup sugar
juice of 1 orange
1¼ cups flour
1 teaspoon ground cinnamon
6 tablespoons butter, at room temperature
½ cup browned pecans, coarsely chopped

Method

Set the oven at 400°F. Butter a shallow ovenproof dish. Cut the rhubarb into 1-inch pieces and lay them in the dish. Sprinkle with ¼ cup of the sugar and the orange juice.

Combine the flour and cinnamon in a bowl and rub in the butter with a fork until the mixture resembles breadcrumbs. Stir in the pecans with the remaining ½ cup sugar and cover the rhubarb with the crumb mixture.

Bake the rhubarb in the preheated oven for 30 minutes or until the fruit is tender and the top is golden brown. Serve at once with a pitcher of cream passed separately.

Rhubarb and Yogurt Pudding

Serves 8

$1\frac{1}{2}$ lb rhubarb, trimmed
$\frac{1}{4}$ cup light brown sugar
$\frac{1}{2}$ teaspoon ground cinnamon
grated rind of $\frac{1}{2}$ orange
1 small carton (8 oz) plain yogurt
$\frac{1}{2}$ cup hazelnuts, toasted, skins removed, and coarsely chopped

Method
Set the oven at 400°F and butter a shallow baking dish. Cut the trimmed rhubarb into 1-inch pieces and lay them in the bottom of the dish. Sprinkle them with the sugar, cinnamon and orange rind. Bake the dish in the preheated oven for 30 minutes or until the rhubarb is tender.

Stir the yogurt with half the hazelnuts and pour this over the rhubarb. Sprinkle with the remaining hazelnuts and return to the oven for 5 minutes. Serve at once.

The rhubarb is trimmed, sprinkled with sugar, cinnamon and orange rind and baked; a topping of yogurt and hazelnuts completes this simply delicious pudding

Festive Peaches

4 peaches
$\frac{1}{4}$ cup raisins
$\frac{1}{4}$ cup chopped dates
$\frac{1}{4}$ cup chopped almonds
2 tablespoons dark brown sugar
2 tablespoons butter, at room temperature
$\frac{1}{4}$ cup honey
heavy cream (for serving)

Method

Remove any stems from the peaches and set them stem side down on your work surface.

Halve the peaches through their equators and remove their pits. Set aside.

Mix the raisins, dates, almonds, brown sugar, soft butter and half the honey together in a bowl. Pile this on one peach half and set the other half on top to reshape them. Set the peaches on a serving dish and spoon a little of the remaining honey over each one. Pass a pitcher of heavy cream when you serve them.

Festive peaches are quick to assemble, easy to serve and good to eat with their date, almond and honey filling. Serve with a pitcher of cream

Swiss Apricots

Serves 8

For jelly roll
$\frac{3}{4}$ cup flour
$\frac{3}{4}$ teaspoon baking powder
pinch of salt
3 eggs
$\frac{3}{4}$ cup sugar
3 tablespoons water
$\frac{1}{2}$ teaspoon vanilla
$\frac{1}{2}$ cup strawberry or raspberry jam, heated until melted

For frosting
12 oz ($1\frac{1}{2}$ large packages) cream cheese
$\frac{1}{4}$ cup sugar
2 tablespoons cream or milk
$\frac{1}{2}$ cup finely chopped browned almonds

For topping
1 can (16 oz) apricots
1 tablespoon apricot jam
$1\frac{1}{2}$ teaspoons arrowroot mixed with 1 tablespoon cold water

11 x 16-inch jelly roll pan or paper case

Method
Set the oven at 375°F. Grease and flour the jelly roll pan or paper case. Sift the flour several times with the baking powder and salt.

Beat the eggs in an electric mixer until completely broken up. Add the sugar gradually and continue beating until the mixture is very thick and light and leaves a ribbon trail on itself when the beaters are lifted. Beat in the water and vanilla.

Sprinkle the flour onto the mixture and beat it only until incorporated. Pour at once into the prepared pan or case and spread evenly with a long metal palette knife. Bake in the preheated oven for 12–15 minutes or until the jelly roll is lightly browned at the edges and firm to the touch in the center.

Turn out the cake, trim it, spread with the melted jam and roll it up from one of the short ends.

Cut the jelly roll into 8 thick slices and set each one cut side up on the work surface.

For the frosting: beat the cream cheese with an electric mixer until soft and light. Beat in the sugar gradually, followed by the cream or milk.

With a small metal spatula, spread the cream cheese mixture on the tops and sides of the jelly roll slices. Press some nuts around the sides.

For topping: drain the apricots into a saucepan. Set the apricots aside and heat the syrup with the apricot jam, whisking until the jam is melted. Strain into a clean saucepan and bring to a boil. Cook 1 minute. Whisk the arrowroot paste into the syrup. Tip into a bowl and leave to cool completely.

Set one apricot on top of each miniature cake and spoon over just enough of the syrup to moisten the fruit only. Refrigerate until serving.

Compote of Prunes

1 box pitted prunes
$1\frac{1}{2}$ cups freshly brewed tea
1 cup water
1 cup red wine
pared rind of 1 lemon
2 tablespoons sugar
6 blanched almonds, split
1 teaspoon arrowroot mixed with 1 tablespoon cold water

Method
Put the prunes in a bowl with the tea, cover with plastic wrap and refrigerate overnight.

Put the water, red wine, lemon rind and sugar into a saucepan and bring slowly to the boil. Lift the prunes from the tea and add them to the red wine mixture. Simmer very gently for 10 minutes or until the prunes are just tender.

Lift the prunes into a serving dish and scatter with the almonds. Remove the lemon rind from the syrup and reduce the syrup until it is 1 cup. Add the arrowroot paste and continue cooking for 1 minute. Pour the sauce over the prunes and leave to cool completely before serving.

Pears in Honey and Lemon

4 large ripe pears
$\frac{1}{2}$ cup honey
$\frac{1}{4}$ cup lemon juice
3 cups water
2-inch piece cinnamon stick
3 cloves
2 tablespoons coarsely chopped walnuts
$\frac{3}{4}$ cup heavy cream (for serving)

Method
Put the honey, lemon juice and water into a saucepan and bring to a boil, stirring occasionally so the honey dissolves.

Peel the pears, leaving them whole with the stalks still attached but remove the eye at the bottom of the pears. Put the pears into the saucepan and add enough additional water to cover all the pears completely. Add the cinnamon stick and cloves.

Return to the boil and simmer gently for 20–30 minutes or until the pears are just tender. Keep turning the pears if they fall onto their sides during cooking.

Drain the pears and stand them upright in a serving dish.

Boil the syrup until it is reduced to 1 cup. Lift out the cinnamon stick and cloves and leave the syrup to cool: stir in the walnuts and pour some of the syrup over each of the pears. Serve them with heavy cream poured over the top just before passing.

Mock mulligatawny soup, made from leftovers, is just as appetizing as the classic recipe

COOKING ON A BUDGET

As the cost of food continues to escalate, we would do well to know how to transform what we happen to have on hand into beautiful and interesting dishes. Rather than making a special trip to the grocery store for soup ingredients, for instance, we should be able to come up with something made from leftovers tucked away in the freezer or with the vegetables that we already have in the refrigerator.

Cooking on a budget always takes a little more time than when preparing luxury cuts of meat which need no disguising of any sort. The dishes that follow are intended as family suppers, and you'll find that if you use your freezer wisely and make the most of everything you've already purchased, these recipes will help stretch your dollar considerably.

Mock Mulligatawny

The real Mulligatawny soup, a dish the English brought back from India, is made with lamb which is cooked with curry and various hot spices. It is a warming and filling dish, and there is an authentic recipe for it in Volume 6. This mock version is a very good facsimile.

1½ cups leftover beef stew or goulash
1 onion, finely chopped
1 tablespoon oil
1 tablespoon curry powder
½ teaspoon ground cumin
1 tart apple, peeled, cored and sliced
1 tablespoon tomato paste
¾ cup beef stock
salt and pepper

To finish
2 cups beef stock
1 teaspoon arrowroot mixed with 1 tablespoon water
1 tablespoon butter
¼ cup heavy cream

Method

Soften the onion in the oil without letting it brown. Add the curry powder and cumin and cook for 1 minute. Add the apple, tomato paste and beef stock and bring to a boil. Add salt and pepper to taste, lower the heat and simmer 10 minutes. Stir in the leftover beef stew or goulash until well mixed in, then work the soup through a food mill, or purée a little at a time in the blender; return to the pan.

To finish: add the beef stock to the soup and bring to a boil. Stir in the arrowroot paste and whisk in the butter. Taste for seasoning and serve at once. Swirl the cream into the top of the soup tureen or on the individual portions.

Cauliflower or Broccoli Cheese Soup

Use the leftovers of either cauliflower or broccoli – or a combination of both – to make this soup.

2 cups leftover cooked chopped cauliflower or broccoli
1 medium onion, finely chopped
2 tablespoons butter
2 leftover cooked potatoes, diced, or 2 medium uncooked potatoes, peeled and diced
1½ cups chicken stock
salt and pepper
1 cup light cream
⅔ cup grated Cheddar cheese
2 tablespoons chopped parsley or fresh chives

Method

Cook the onion in the butter until soft but not brown. Add the cauliflower or broccoli and the diced potatoes. Add 1 cup of the chicken stock. Bring to a boil and simmer 2 minutes if potatoes are cooked, or 5 minutes if potatoes are uncooked. Work the soup in a blender, a little at a time, then return to the saucepan and stir in the remaining stock, salt and pepper, and light cream. Return to the boil, taste for seasoning and take the pan from the heat. Add the grated cheese a little at a time and sprinkle the top with the parsley or chives. Serve at once.

Carrot Soup

2 cups diced leftover cooked carrots and potatoes, mixed
1 onion, finely chopped
2 tablespoons butter
1½ cups chicken stock
salt and pepper
4 stalks of celery, trimmed and finely chopped
1 cup half and half
2 tablespoons chopped fresh mint or parsley

Method

Cook the onion in the butter until soft and brown. Pour in the chicken stock with salt and pepper to taste and the chopped celery. Bring to a boil, lower the heat and simmer 10 minutes. Add the carrots and potatoes and simmer another 5 minutes.

Work the soup a little at a time in a blender, then strain it into a clean saucepan, pressing the contents of the strainer well to remove as much of the vegetables as possible.

Stir in the half and half and return the soup just to the boil. Sprinkle the fresh mint or parsley on top and serve at once.

Watercress Soup

stalks from 1 bunch fresh watercress, chopped
5 outside leaves from a Romaine or Boston lettuce, shredded
2 leftover cooked broccoli stalks, diced
1 onion, finely chopped
2 tablespoons butter
1¼ cups fresh white breadcrumbs
1½ cups chicken stock
1 cup light cream
salt and pepper

Method

Combine the watercress stalks, lettuce leaves and broccoli in a bowl and set aside.

Cook the onion in the butter until soft but not brown. Stir the breadcrumbs into the pan, then pour in the stock with the green vegetables. Bring to a boil and simmer 2 minutes.

Purée the soup a little at a time in the blender, then return it to a clean saucepan. Add the light cream with salt and pepper and taste for seasoning. Serve at once.

Green Pea Soup
To the recipe for Watercress soup above, add 2 cup cooked peas and garnish with some freshly chopped mint.

This creamy Cauliflower cheese soup takes very little time to make and, with a freshly baked Wholewheat roll (see recipe on page 54), would make a filling lunch-time snack on a cold day

Basic Meat Sauce

3 lb lean ground beef
½ tablespoon oil
2 large onions, finely chopped
3 tablespoons flour
5 cups stock
salt and pepper

Method

Break up the ground beef with your hands and set aside. Heat a large heavy-based flameproof casserole and add the oil. When hot, add the ground beef and stir over a high heat until the beef is all separated and browned. If the meat has produced a lot of fat, lift it out with a large metal spoon as you tip the casserole so it all falls to one end.

Add the onion to the pan and continue cooking over a high heat until the onion is slightly softened. Sprinkle in the flour and stir it well until it is completely absorbed by the meat. Pour in the stock with salt and pepper to taste and bring to a boil.

Cover and simmer gently, stirring occasionally, for 2 hours or until the mixture is thick and well-flavored.

Note: One of the most practical ways to store meat sauce in this quantity would be to divide it into three 1 lb portions and pack it in three freezer containers so defrosting the portions later would be very simple.

Italian Meat Sauce with Pasta

1 lb portion of cooked meat sauce
1 medium onion, finely chopped
1 tablespoon butter
¾ cup tomato sauce (see page 91) or 1 can (8 oz) Italian-style plum tomatoes
1 clove of garlic, crushed
salt and pepper
2 cups elbow macaroni
½ cup freshly grated Parmesan cheese

Method

Soften the onion in the butter in a large skillet until the onion is transparent but not brown. Stir in the tomato sauce or whole tomatoes with the garlic and plenty of salt and pepper to taste. If using whole tomatoes, crush them in the pan with a fork. Bring to a boil, cover partially with the lid, and lower the heat. Cook, stirring, for 15 minutes or until the mixture is quite pulpy.

Meanwhile, bring a very large saucepan of water to the boil and sprinkle in the macaroni. Return to the boil and cook steadily for 12–15 minutes or until the pasta is just done. Drain, rinse with hot water, and drain again. Return to the saucepan and pour in the tomato sauce. Stir well and taste for seasoning.

Butter a deep wide ovenproof dish and set the oven at 400°F.

Spoon the macaroni into the bottom of the dish and pile the meat sauce on top. Sprinkle with the grated Parmesan and bake in the preheated oven for 15 minutes or until the top is browned and the sauce is bubbling at the edges.

Hungarian Meat Sauce

1 lb portion of cooked meat sauce
4 medium zucchini
4 tablespoons butter
1 tablespoon paprika
1 onion, finely chopped
3 tablespoons white wine vinegar
¼ teaspoon caraway seeds
1 teaspoon sugar
kneaded butter made with 1½ tablespoons butter and 1 tablespoon flour
salt and pepper

Method

Butter an ovenproof dish and set the oven at 350°F.

Spread the meat sauce in the dish and cover with foil. Bake in the preheated oven for 12 minutes or until hot.

Peel the zucchini and cut it into quarters. Scoop out the seeds and slice the strips thinly. Melt 3 tablespoons of the butter in a skillet and sauté the zucchini briskly for 4 minutes, shaking the pan constantly. Sprinkle in the paprika and stir well. Remove the zucchini from the pan and add the remaining butter. Cook the onion until soft but not brown, then add the vinegar, caraway seeds and sugar. Thicken this mixture with the kneaded butter, replace the zucchini, season with salt and pepper, cover and simmer for 5 minutes. Spoon the marrow over the meat sauce in the baking dish and serve at once.

Another variation: cover Basic meat sauce with a purée of potatoes and bake a cottage pie

Quiches Variées

Pastry for two quiches
3 cups flour
pinch of salt
$\frac{3}{4}$ cup butter, cut up
4 tablespoons shortening
2 egg yolks
$\frac{1}{3}$ cup ice water

Custard for 2 quiches
4 eggs
2 egg yolks
1 cup grated Swiss cheese
salt and pepper
$2\frac{1}{2}$ cups light cream
2 tablespoons butter
2 medium onions, finely chopped

Filling for first quiche
5 strips bacon
2 slices Canadian bacon
$\frac{1}{4}$ cup diced Gruyère cheese

Filling for second quiche
1 can (8 oz) whole tomatoes
1 clove of garlic, crushed
$\frac{1}{2}$ cup freshly grated Parmesan cheese

Two 8-inch deep quiche pans

Method

For the pastry: sift the flour with the salt into a bowl. Add the butter and shortening and cut it into the flour with a long metal palette knife until the mixture looks like breadcrumbs. Aerate the dough by lifting it up and down with your hands, then stir in the egg yolks and water all at once and stir with the palette knife to form a dough. Knead lightly on a floured board until smooth. Wrap in plastic film and refrigerate for 30 minutes.

Set the oven at 375°F.

Divide the pastry in half and roll each half out and line one of the quiche pans. Bake them blind in the preheated oven for 15 minutes or until just set. Remove the foil and beans and leave them to cool slightly. Leave the oven on.

For the custard mixture: beat the eggs and yolks in a bowl with the grated cheese, salt and pepper, and the light cream. Melt the butter in a skillet and cook the onions until soft but not brown. Stir it into the egg mixture.

For the first quiche: cook the bacon in a skillet until it is golden and has rendered all its fat. Remove the bacon from the pan and leave to cool slightly; then crush it with your fingers into $\frac{1}{2}$-inch pieces. Discard all but 1 tablespoon of fat from the pan. Cut the Canadian bacon into thin strips and sauté them quickly in the hot fat for 2 minutes, shaking the pan constantly. Lift and leave to cool slightly.

Lay both kinds of bacon in the bottom of one of the quiches and pour in half the custard mixture. Scatter the diced Gruyère cheese on top.

For the second quiche: pile the tomatoes into a saucepan and crush them with a fork. Add the garlic and bring to a boil. Cook, stirring, over a low heat for 5 minutes or until the mixture is pulpy. Stir this tomato sauce into the remaining custard and pour into the second quiche. Sprinkle the top with the grated Parmesan.

Bake the quiches in the preheated oven for 30 minutes or until they are just set. Take from the oven and leave to cool slightly. Then cut into wedges for serving.

Note: each quiche will serve 4 and can be frozen.

Pizzas

Basic dough for two pizzas
1 envelope dried yeast or 1 cake compressed yeast
2 tablespoons lukewarm water
1 teaspoon sugar
1 teaspoon salt
1 cup boiling water
$\frac{1}{4}$ cup shortening
3 cups flour
few drops oil (for greasing bowl and pans)

Shrimp and mushroom topping
$\frac{1}{2}$ lb uncooked shrimps, shelled
4 tablespoons butter
$\frac{1}{2}$ lb mushrooms, thickly sliced
1 shallot, finely chopped
salt and pepper
$\frac{1}{2}$ lb Mozzarella cheese, grated
$\frac{1}{2}$ cup freshly grated Parmesan cheese

Italian sausage and anchovy topping
$\frac{3}{4}$ cup thick tomato sauce (see page 91)
1 clove of garlic, crushed
1 onion, finely chopped
salt and pepper
$\frac{1}{2}$ lb Italian sausages
$\frac{1}{2}$ lb Mozzarella cheese, grated
2 cans anchovy fillets, drained
$\frac{1}{2}$ cup freshly grated Parmesan cheese

Two 10-inch pizza pans

Method

Make the pizza dough (see Vol 8, page 127). Leave it to rise in a warm place until doubled in bulk.

Prepare the toppings.

For the shrimp and mushroom topping: melt 2 tablespoons of the butter in a skillet and sauté the shrimps over a high heat for 3 minutes until they turn bright pink. Remove them with a spoon and add the remaining 2 tablespoons butter to the pan. Sauté the mushrooms over a high heat for 1 minute, add the shallot with salt and pepper to taste and continue cooking until all the moisture in the mushrooms evaporates. Set the mushrooms aside while you prepare the other topping.

For the sausage and anchovy topping: combine the tomato sauce, garlic and onion with plenty of salt and pepper to taste in a small saucepan. Bring to a boil, lower the heat, and cook for 5 minutes, stirring occasionally. Meanwhile, prick the sausages in several places and fry them in a skillet until golden brown. Pour in $\frac{1}{4}$ cup water and continue cooking until the water has completely evaporated, shaking the pan constantly so the sausages turn in the liquid.

To assemble the pizzas: set the oven at 425°F. Use the few drops of oil to lightly grease the pizza pans.

Divide the pizza dough in half and roll each half out to a 10-inch round. Lift them into the pizza pans.

For the shrimp topping: sprinkle one of the rounds of dough with the Mozzarella cheese, cut the shrimps in half and lay them on the cheese. Sprinkle them with the mushrooms and then dust with the Parmesan cheese.

For the sausage topping: spread the tomato sauce on the other round of dough and sprinkle it with the Mozzarella cheese. Lay the anchovies on the cheese like the spokes of a wheel. Cut each sausage into several slices and scatter them on the round. Sprinkle with the Parmesan cheese.

Without letting the dough rise, bake the pizzas in the preheated oven for 20 minutes, or until the dough is puffed and firm and all the cheese has melted.

Note: each pizza serves 4 and freezes well.

Savory Pains Perdus

'Pain perdu' is not unlike our French toast and it was originally invented as a way to use bread (pain) that was lost (perdu) for kitchen use because it had become stale. The method below wraps the dipped slices of bread around savory fillings before baking in a hot oven until browned and crisp. These are light supper dishes which will use up the meat and trimmings from a large gathering or holiday dinner.

8 thin slices firm white bread
$\frac{1}{2}$ cup half and half
2 eggs, beaten to mix with salt and pepper
4 tablespoons butter, melted
Serves 4

Method
Set the oven at 400°F and generously butter a long ovenproof dish. Have the chosen filling all prepared.

Remove the crusts from the bread and roll each slice firmly with a rolling pin. Dip each one first in the half and half and then in the beaten egg. Leave bread for 10 seconds so it softens.

Place a spoonful of the chosen filling on the bread and roll the slice up firmly. Place, seamed side down, in the ovenproof dish and brush all the rolls well with the melted butter.

Bake them in the preheated oven for 40–45 minutes or until browned and crisp. Serve at once.

Ham Filling

8 slices boiled ham
2 teaspoons Dijon-style mustard
black pepper

Method
Spread each ham slice with some mustard and sprinkle with black pepper. Place the ham on the prepared bread and roll up and bake as above.

Lamb Filling

1 cup cooked shredded lamb
1 tablespoon Worcestershire sauce
1 tablespoon ketchup
1 onion, thinly sliced
1 tablespoon butter
2 tomatoes, scalded, peeled, seeded and cut into strips
salt and pepper
2 tablespoons grated Cheddar cheese

Method
Combine the strips of lamb in a bowl with the Worcestershire sauce and ketchup and leave to marinate for 30 minutes.

Soften the onion in the butter and cook until transparent but not colored. Stir in the strips of tomato with salt and pepper to taste and remove from the heat. Stir the onion and tomato mixture into the lamb mixture with the cheese and taste for seasoning.

Divide the lamb filling among the 8 slices of bread and roll up each one. Bake as directed above.

Beef Filling

8 very thin slices cooked roast beef
2 teaspoons prepared horseradish
1 teaspoon prepared hot mustard

Method
Lay a slice of the cooked beef on each piece of prepared bread and spread them with the horseradish and dot each with a touch of mustard. Roll up and bake as directed above.

Pork Filling

1 cup finely chopped cooked pork
$\frac{1}{4}$ cup leftover pork stuffing
2 tablespoons cream
1 tablespoon mango chutney
1 tablespoon applesauce

Method
Mix the chopped pork with the leftover stuffing and work in the cream to soften the mixture to a spreadable consistency. Stir in the chutney with the applesauce.

Spread some of the filling on the slices of prepared bread and roll up and bake as directed above.

Chicken Filling

1 cup diced cooked chicken
2 tablespoons butter
1 medium onion, finely sliced
$\frac{1}{2}$ teaspoon paprika
pinch of cayenne pepper
pinch of ground cumin
salt

Method
Melt the butter in a skillet and cook the onion until soft but not brown. Add the paprika, cayenne pepper and cumin and cook 1 minute to mellow the spices. Add the chicken with salt to taste and stir well until it is all coated with the spicy mixture.

Divide the mixture among the 8 slices of bread. Roll up and bake as directed above.

Cheese Filling

16 very thin slices Swiss cheese
2 teaspoons Dijon-style mustard
2 tablespoons capers

Method
Trim any rind, if necessary, from the slices of cheese and spread 8 slices with some mustard. Scatter a few capers on top and set the other slices on top. Put the double slices of cheese on the prepared bread and roll up and bake as directed above.

Savory Choux Ring

scant 1 cup flour
salt and pepper
1 cup water
$\frac{1}{2}$ cup butter, cut up
4 eggs, beaten to mix
$\frac{1}{2}$ cup freshly grated Parmesan cheese
1 teaspoon Dijon-style mustard
2 slices Canadian bacon, cut into dice

9-inch ring mold

Method

Set the oven at 400°F and grease the ring mold.

Sift the flour onto a sheet of waxed paper. Add salt and pepper to taste. Bring the water and butter to a rolling boil, remove from the heat and shoot in the flour all at once. Beat with a wooden spoon until the mixture forms a ball in the middle of the pan, then return to the heat for 1 minute to evaporate any excess moisture.

Beat in the eggs a little at a time, then beat in the Parmesan cheese, mustard and diced bacon. Spoon the mixture into the prepared ring mold.

Bake the choux ring in the preheated oven for 30 minutes. Turn the temperature down to 350°F and continue baking for another 30 minutes.

Turn out onto a wire rack and fill with either of the following fillings: to do this, split the ring in half horizontally while hot, spoon the chosen filling into the bottom half and set the top on again.

Serve at once, cut into thick portions.

Chicken and Mushroom Filling

2 cups cooked chicken, cut into shreds
1 onion, finely chopped
2 tablespoons butter
$\frac{1}{2}$ lb mushrooms, quartered
salt and pepper
1 tablespoon flour
$\frac{3}{4}$ cup chicken stock

Method

Fry the onion in the butter until soft but not brown. Add the mushrooms with salt and pepper to taste and continue frying over a fairly high heat until the mushrooms release their liquid. Then keep stirring until the liquid in the pan evaporates. Sprinkle in the flour and stir until it starts to brown. Then add the stock and bring to a boil, stirring constantly. Add the shredded chicken, taste for seasoning and use as directed in the choux ring recipe.

Bacon and Egg Filling

$\frac{1}{2}$ lb Canadian bacon, cut into strips
6 eggs
béchamel sauce made with 3 tablespoons butter, 3 tablespoons flour, $1\frac{1}{4}$ cups infused milk
2 medium onions, thinly sliced
2 tablespoons butter
$\frac{1}{2}$ cup heavy cream
salt and pepper

Method

Bring a large saucepan of water to the boil, remove from the heat and gently lower in the eggs. Replace the pan on the heat and bring to a boil; lower the heat so the water is bubbling gently and cook the eggs for 12 minutes exactly. Lift from the water and set in a bowl of very cold water. Peel the eggs and chop them coarsely.

Prepare the béchamel sauce and set aside.

Fry the onions in the butter until soft but not brown. Add the strips of bacon and continue cooking for another 2 minutes, shaking the pan constantly over a high heat. Stir the contents of the pan into the béchamel sauce with the cream and return to the boil. Add salt and pepper to taste and spoon into the choux ring as directed in the recipe on this page.

Potato Galette with Sausage Filling

Most molded potato dishes are made from thinly sliced or shredded uncooked potatoes, but this one uses cooked potato purée which is sandwiched with a sausage filling.

1½ lb boiling potatoes
salt and pepper
2 tablespoons butter
1 teaspoon Dijon-style mustard
¼ cup grated Cheddar cheese
2 tablespoons hot milk
2 eggs, beaten to mix
2 tablespoons dried breadcrumbs

For filling
2 large onions, finely chopped
3 tablespoons butter
½ lb loose pork sausage

8-inch round cake pan

Method

Peel and quarter the potatoes and put them into a saucepan with water to cover them. Bring slowly to the boil, cover and simmer for 15 minutes or until the potatoes are very tender. Drain them and work them through a food mill back into the saucepan. Stir over a low heat for 1 minute to remove any excess moisture from them. Take from the heat and beat in salt and pepper to taste with half the butter. Add the mustard and cheese with the hot milk and eggs; beat well to mix.

Use the remaining 1 tablespoon butter to grease the cake pan and dust it with the dried breadcrumbs. Set the oven at 375°F.

For the filling: cook the onions slowly in the butter until they are soft and golden brown. This will take about 15 minutes. Break up the sausage meat with your hands and add it to the onions in the pan. Turn up the heat slightly and fry the mixture, stirring constantly, for 10 minutes or until it is well browned. Pile into a colander to drain.

Put half the potato mixture into the prepared pan and pile the sausage and onion filling on top. Smooth it with the back of a wet metal spoon and cover with the remaining potato mixture. Smooth the top of the potato mixture and set the pan in the preheated oven. Bake the galette for 45 minutes or until well browned on the top. Remove from the oven and leave for 5 minutes to cool slightly.

Turn the galette out onto a round platter and cut into wedges for serving with braised cabbage (see Vol 21) and a spicy apple and tomato sauce.

Spicy Apple and Tomato Sauce

1 tablespoon butter
1 medium onion, sliced
1 large cooking apple
1 teaspoon paprika
2 tablespoons tomato paste
1 cup chicken stock
dash of Tabasco sauce
1 tablespoon sugar
1 clove of garlic, crushed
salt and pepper
½ bay leaf

Method

Melt the butter in a saucepan and cook the onion until soft but not brown. Peel, core and slice the apple and stir it into the onion with the paprika, tomato paste, stock, Tabasco, sugar, garlic, salt and pepper and bay leaf. Stir well and bring to a boil. Simmer for 15 minutes or until the sauce is pulpy.

Work it through a food mill into a clean saucepan, bring just to a boil, taste for seasoning and serve.

Mushroom and Bacon Filling for Potato Galette

1 lb mushrooms
1 tablespoon butter
4 slices of bacon, cut into strips
6 large celery stalks, trimmed and finely sliced
1 shallot, finely chopped
1 teaspoon chopped mixed herbs (marjoram, tarragon, basil)
salt and pepper

Method

Trim the mushroom stems level with the caps. Finely chop the stems and thinly slice the caps.

Melt the butter in a skillet and cook the bacon until the fat begins to run. Turn up the heat, add the celery and cook until the celery begins to brown. Lift out. Add the chopped mushrooms to the pan with the shallot and mixed herbs and cook slowly until the mushrooms release their liquid. Cook over a high heat until most of the liquid evaporates. Add the sliced mushrooms and cook over a high heat for several minutes. Stir in the celery mixture and add plenty of salt and pepper to taste.

Sandwich this filling between two layers of potato purée as directed in the Potato galette recipe and bake according to the same directions.

The Potato galette with sausage filling is served with braised cabbage and accompanied by a Spicy tomato and apple sauce. Pass a bottle of Chianti with this hearty dish

Vegetable Fritto Misto

Choose 4 vegetables:
parsnips and walnuts, spinach, cauliflower, beets, Brussels sprouts, mushrooms, onions, fresh herbs (parsley, marjoram, thyme)

To prepare vegetables
1 tablespoon butter
1 egg, separated
salt and pepper
vinaigrette dressing (made with 4 tablespoons white wine vinegar, salt and pepper, dry mustard, generous $\frac{3}{4}$ cup oil)
about $1\frac{1}{2}$ cups flour seasoned with salt and pepper
Italian tomato sauce (for serving)

For fritter batter
2 cups flour
large pinch of salt
1 envelope dried yeast or 1 cake compressed yeast
2 cups warm water
2 tablespoons oil
deep fat (for frying)

Method

For the fritter batter: sift the flour and salt into a bowl. Add the yeast, warm water and oil and stir the batter to make the consistency of thick cream. Beat well for a minute, then cover with plastic film and leave in a warm place for 15–20 or until well risen.

Prepare the chosen vegetables and heat deep fat for frying just before serving.

Parsnips and walnuts: peel parsnips and slice. Put into a saucepan with water to cover and bring to a boil; simmer for 15 minutes or until they are tender. Drain and work through a food mill into a bowl. Beat in 1 tablespoon butter and an egg yolk with salt and pepper to taste. Leave to cool. Working on a floured board with floured hands, divide the mixture into walnut-sized pieces and roll them into balls. Press a walnut half carefully on one side of each ball, then dip them into the fritter batter and deep fat fry until golden.

Spinach: remove the leaves from the stems and wash the greens well. Drop into a pan of boiling water and drain at once. Add salt and pepper and enough vinaigrette dressing to coat the leaves and leave to marinate for several minutes. Take several leaves at a time and roll them into cigar shapes. Coat with the seasoned flour and dip into the fritter batter. Deep fat fry until golden.

Cauliflower: remove the cauliflowerets from the stem and drop into a pan of boiling water. Cook for 5 minutes or until just tender; drain. Add enough vinaigrette dressing to moisten them and leave to marinate for several minutes. Dip into the fritter batter and deep fat fry until golden.

Beets: boil the beets in their skins for 45 minutes or until just tender. Drain and slip off skins. Slice the beets and marinate for 10 minutes in enough vinaigrette dressing to moisten them. Pat dry with paper toweling, roll in seasoned flour, dip into fritter batter and fry in deep fat until golden.

Brussels sprouts: trim stems from Brussels sprouts and mark an 'x' in the stem end. Drop into a pan of boiling water and return to the boil. Simmer 4 minutes or until just tender. Drain and roll in seasoned flour, then dip into fritter batter. Deep fat fry until golden.

Mushrooms: marinate the mushrooms for 30 minutes in enough vinaigrette dressing to moisten them. Pat dry and roll in seasoned flour. Dip into fritter batter and deep fat fry until golden.

Onions: choose large Spanish onions and cut them into $\frac{1}{4}$-inch thick rings. Push through each ring so slices fall apart and set them on a large plate. One by one, dip rings into egg white and then into seasoned flour and return to the plate. Deep fat fry until golden.

Herbs: tie the herbs together at the stem with string. Dip the leafy end into fritter batter and still holding onto the string, fry the bouquet in the deep fat until golden brown. Remove string and use herbs to garnish the platter of fritto misto.

Serve with Italian tomato sauce.

Italian Tomato Sauce

2 tablespoons butter
1 medium onion, finely chopped
1 medium carrot, finely chopped
1 can (28 oz) Italian-style plum tomatoes
1 cup chicken stock
1 bay leaf
1 clove of garlic, crushed
salt and pepper

Method

Melt the butter in a saucepan and cook the onion and carrot until soft but not brown. Crush the tomatoes in your hands as you add them to the pan. Pour in the chicken stock, add the bay leaf and crushed garlic with salt and pepper to taste.

Bring to a boil, lower the heat, cover and simmer for 30 minutes or until the sauce is very pulpy. Work the mixture through a food mill into a clean pan, taste for seasoning, return to the boil and serve as an accompaniment to Vegetable fritto misto.

Pork Milanaise

3 cups diced cooked pork
1 tablespoon oil
1 onion, sliced
1 clove of garlic, crushed
$\frac{1}{4}$ lb mushrooms, halved
1 can (1 lb) whole tomatoes
$1\frac{1}{4}$ cups chicken stock
2 teaspoons tomato paste
$\frac{1}{2}$ teaspoon dried basil
salt and pepper
$\frac{1}{4}$ cup capers, drained

Method

Heat the oil in a large skillet and sauté the onion until soft but not brown. Add the garlic with the mushrooms and cook them until they release their moisture. Continue cooking over a high heat, stirring occasionally, until the moisture is evaporated. Add the tomatoes, crushing them in your hand as they go into the pan, pour in the stock, tomato paste, basil, salt and pepper to taste and bring to a boil.

Lower the heat and simmer gently for 15 minutes or until the mixture is pulpy. Add the diced pork with the capers, stir the contents of the pan well to mix everything and continue cooking for 5 minutes or until the pork is very hot. Taste for seasoning and serve at once.

Pork milanaise – an excellent way to stretch leftover meat

Pork Dumplings

Whole onions are stuffed with ground pork and chestnuts and wrapped in pastry to make these dumplings.

4 large onions
1 cup ground cooked pork
$\frac{1}{4}$ cup applesauce
6 chestnuts, slit, boiled until tender and chopped
pinch of ground cloves
salt and pepper
2 cup quantity rough puff pastry (see Vol 2)
1 egg, beaten to mix (for glaze)

Method

Peel the onions but trim away the brown part of the root, leaving the white part of the root intact. Put the onions into a large saucepan with water to cover them and bring to a boil. Simmer gently for 15 minutes or until the onions are slightly soft. Drain and rinse with cold water.

Without cutting through the root, remove the center of each onion to make them hollow. Use a small sharp knife or a grapefruit knife to do this. Mix the ground pork with the applesauce, chopped chestnuts, cloves and salt and pepper to taste. Divide the mixture among the hollow onions and pack it in as tightly as possible.

Roll out the rough puff pastry to a 14-inch square and cut the square into quarters. Brush the pastry edges with the beaten egg and place an onion in the center of each one. Bring the edges up to enclose the onions, cutting away any overlapping pastry. Use the trimmings to make leaves on the top. Set the dumplings on a lightly greased and dampened baking sheet and refrigerate for 15 minutes.

Meanwhile, set the oven at 425°F. Brush each dumpling with egg glaze and bake them in the preheated oven for 15 minutes. Reduce the oven temperature to 350°F and continue baking for another 45 minutes, or until the pastry is nicely browned and a skewer poked through into the onion and stuffing is very hot to the touch when withdrawn.

Pork and Lentil Curry

- 2 cups diced cooked pork
- 1 tablespoon oil
- 1 large onion, finely chopped
- 2 medium potatoes, peeled and cubed
- 1 clove of garlic, crushed
- $\frac{1}{2}$ teaspoon cayenne
- 1 teaspoon salt
- 1 teaspoon turmeric
- 1 teaspoon ground ginger
- 1 teaspoon ground coriander
- 1 teaspoon cinnamon
- $\frac{1}{4}$ teaspoon ground cloves
- 1 bay leaf
- 1 cup lentils
- 3 cups water
- 1 package (10 oz) frozen green peas, thawed

Method

Heat the oil in a large skillet and cook the onion until soft but not brown. Add the potato and garlic with the cayenne, salt, turmeric, ginger, coriander, cinnamon and cloves and stir well.

Add the bay leaf, lentils and water and bring to the boil. Cover and simmer very gently for 15 minutes or until the lentils are soft. Add the pork and thawed peas to the pan, stir well, return to the boil and continue cooking for another 5 minutes or until everything is thoroughly heated. Taste for seasoning and serve at once.

Chili Pork Salad

- 1 can (1 lb) red kidney beans, drained
- 3 cups diced cold pork
- salt and pepper
- 2 large oranges, peeled and cut into sections
- 1 bunch watercress, washed and chopped
- 2 stalks celery, trimmed and chopped
- $\frac{1}{4}$ cup oil
- 1 tablespoon lemon juice
- 1 tablespoon white wine vinegar
- 1 tablespoon chopped fresh chives
- 1 fresh chili, seeded and chopped or $\frac{1}{4}$ teaspoon ground chili peppers
- small head of bibb lettuce (for serving)

Method

Combine the kidney beans, pork, salt and pepper, and orange segments in a bowl. Add the watercress and celery and stir everything well.

Whisk the oil with the lemon juice, vinegar, chives and chopped chili or ground chili and pour over the salad just before serving. Toss well, taste for seasoning and serve on a bed of lettuce with some crusty bread and butter.

Chili pork salad – some unusual ingredients combine to make this cold dish

Beef Yorky

3 cups diced cooked roast beef
1 small onion
1 tablespoon curry powder
1 tablespoon tomato paste
1 small gherkin pickle
salt and pepper
1 egg, beaten

For batter
1 cup flour
pinch of salt
1 teaspoon paprika
1 egg, beaten to mix
¾ cup milk
¾ cup water
2 tablespoons beef drippings or oil

Method

Grind the beef and onion together and stir in the curry powder and tomato paste. Chop the gherkin, add it to the beef with salt and pepper and enough beaten egg to bind the mixture. Shape it into 24 small balls and set them on a plate.

Set the oven at 425°F and take out a small roasting pan large enough to hold the roast beef balls.

For the batter: sift the flour, salt and paprika into a bowl and make a well in the center. Add the egg and milk and stir the ingredients in the well until they are smooth. Gradually stir in the flour until it is all incorporated, then add the water and beat well until the mixture is completely smooth.

Put the drippings or oil in the roasting tin and set it in the preheated oven for a few minutes or until the fat is very hot. Quickly pour in the batter and set the balls in it.

Bake for 40 minutes or until puffed and golden brown. Serve at once.

Chinese-style Beef

3 cups shredded cooked roast beef
¼ cup peanut oil
1 onion, thinly sliced
2 stalks celery, trimmed and thinly sliced
¼ lb mushrooms, sliced
¾ lb fresh Chinese noodles, cooked and drained
¼ cup soy sauce
1 tablespoon Worcestershire sauce
¾ cup stock
½ cup thinly sliced bamboo shoots
salt and pepper

Method

Heat the oil in a wok or very large skillet and sauté the onion and celery for 1 minute. Add the mushrooms and cook another minute.

Add the beef and continue cooking, stirring constantly, until it is covered with the oil, then add the noodles, soy sauce and Worcestershire sauce and toss well. Pour in the stock with the bamboo shoots and salt and pepper to taste and bring just to the boil. Cook for 3 minutes, stirring, or until the contents are very hot, then taste for seasoning and serve at once.

Swedish Meat Balls

2 cups ground cooked beef
½ lb ground uncooked pork
1 egg, beaten to mix
1 cup milk
¾ cup dry white breadcrumbs
2 tablespoons finely chopped onion
3 tablespoons butter, melted
1 teaspoon salt
pepper
¼ teaspoon ground mace
2 tablespoons flour
1 cup stock
¾ cup light cream

Method

Mix the ground beef and pork together. Then mix the egg, milk and breadcrumbs. Set aside for a few minutes so the breadcrumbs can absorb the liquid in the bowl. Stir the onion, 1 tablespoon of the butter, the salt, pepper and mace into the breadcrumb mixture, then add the meat and mix with your hands until smooth. Shape the mixture into small balls.

Heat the remaining 2 tablespoons butter in a skillet and fry the meatballs until browned all over. Tip the pan to one side and spoon out the fat from the bottom of the pan. Sprinkle the meatballs with the flour and pour in the stock. Bring just to the boil, turn the heat down, cover and simmer for 35 minutes, or until the meatballs are very firm to the touch and a skewer inserted into the middle is hot to the touch when withdrawn. Add the cream, shake the pan to distribute it, and taste the liquid for seasoning. Serve at once.

Roast Beef Salad

3 cups roast beef cut into strips
½ cup olive oil
¼ cup white wine vinegar
2 tablespoons prepared horseradish
½ teaspoon dry mustard
few drops of Worcestershire sauce
1 dill pickle, coarsely chopped
2 tablespoons capers, drained
1 tablespoon chopped fresh parsley
salt and pepper
bunch of watercress (for garnish)

Method

Whisk the olive oil with the vinegar, horseradish, mustard, and Worcestershire sauce. Pour over the strips of roast beef in a bowl and cover tightly with plastic film. Leave to marinate for 3 hours, stirring occasionally.

Add the chopped pickle, capers, parsley and salt and pepper to taste and stir well to combine the ingredients. Arrange the salad in a bowl and garnish with sprigs of watercress. Serve with a potato salad or coleslaw and some dark bread and butter.

Turkey (or Chicken) Lasagne

4 cups cooked turkey or chicken, cut into strips
6 tablespoons butter
$\frac{1}{2}$ lb mushrooms, sliced
1 10-oz package frozen leaf spinach, cooked and drained
pinch of grated nutmeg
salt and pepper
$\frac{1}{3}$ cup flour
$1\frac{1}{2}$ cups milk
$1\frac{1}{4}$ cups chicken stock
1 cup grated Cheddar cheese
12 long strips green lasagne

12-inch diameter baking dish

Method

Remove any bones or skin from the turkey or chicken and set aside. Set the oven at 400°F.

Melt 2 tablespoons of the butter in a skillet and fry the mushrooms over a high heat for 3 minutes. Add the drained spinach and stir well. Season with nutmeg and plenty of salt and pepper to taste, set aside.

Melt the remaining 4 tablespoons butter in a saucepan and stir in the flour. Cook for 2 minutes or until the roux is a pale straw-color, then stir in the milk and stock and bring to a boil, whisking constantly. Simmer for 2 minutes, then take from the heat and add all but $\frac{1}{4}$ cup of the cheese with salt and pepper to taste.

Butter a 12-inch baking dish and spread the mushrooms and spinach mixture in the bottom of the dish. Add a few spoonfuls of the sauce. Set aside.

Bring a large stockpot of water to the boil and cook the lasagne for 12 minutes or until just tender. Drain, pat dry with a clean kitchen towel and place half the lasagne over the sauce in the dish.

Cover with the turkey or chicken strips and pour over half the remaining sauce. Set the remaining lasagne strips on top and cover with the remaining sauce. Sprinkle the rest of the cheese on top and bake the lasagne in the preheated oven for 30 minutes or until bubbling at the edges and browned on the top.

Cut into squares for serving.

Swedish meat balls (top) are served with slices of onion and a bowl of red cabbage with apple. The turkey for the lasagne (below) is sandwiched between layers of pasta and spinach, and topped with cheese. Cut it into squares for serving

Lamb with Apricots

4 cups diced cooked lamb
1 tablespoon oil
1 onion, finely chopped
1 cup long-grain white rice
1 cup dried apricots, soaked overnight in water to cover
2 tablespoons honey
salt and pepper
½ 10-oz package frozen peas, thawed

Method

Remove any fat from the lamb and set aside. Set the oven at 350°F.

Heat the oil in a flameproof casserole and sauté the onion until soft but not brown. Add the rice and stir until all the grains are completely mixed in. Drain the apricot soaking liquid into a large measuring cup and add enough water to make 2½ cups. Stir the water into the casserole and bring to a boil. Add the apricots, honey, and salt and pepper to taste. Cover with the lid and cook in the preheated oven for 25 minutes or until the rice is tender. Remove the lid and stir in the peas carefully with a fork. Recover the casserole and cook for another 5 minutes or until the peas are very hot.

Lamb with apricots, peas and rice (left) and Lamb and spinach moussaka (right) are two imaginative ways of stretching small quantities of meat left over from a large roast

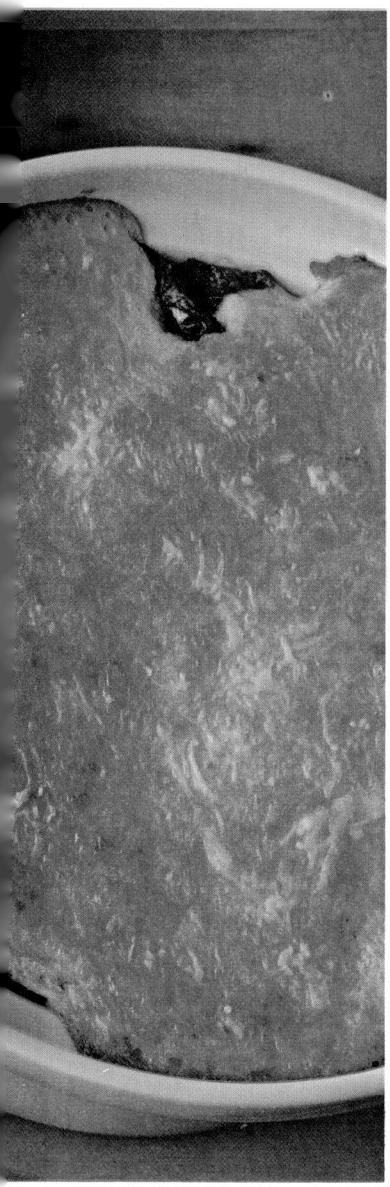

Lamb and Spinach Moussaka

1½ lb cooked lamb, ground
1 tablespoon oil
1 medium onion, sliced
1½ cups stock
1 teaspoon Worcestershire sauce
1 tablespoon tomato paste
salt and pepper
2 x 10 oz packages frozen leaf spinach, thawed
2 tablespoons butter, melted
pinch of ground nutmeg
1 can (1 lb) tomatoes, crushed

For topping
1 small container (8 oz) plain yogurt
1 tablespoon flour
1 egg
½ cup grated Cheddar cheese
salt and pepper

Method

Heat the oil and sauté the onion until soft. Add the meat and continue to cook until it is broken up and beginning to brown. Add the stock, Worcestershire sauce and tomato paste and bring to a boil. Simmer 5 minutes. Add salt and pepper to taste.

Mix the spinach with the butter and nutmeg. Season well.

Generously butter an ovenproof dish and pour in a layer of meat, a layer of tomatoes and a layer of spinach. Do another layer of each one. For the topping: whisk the yogurt, flour, egg, and half the cheese together. Add salt and pepper and spread it over the filling.

To freeze Leave the casserole in the freezer until frozen, then cover.

Thawing and serving Let the casserole defrost completely in the refrigerator for 24 hours. Preheat the oven to 350°F. Sprinkle the top with the remaining cheese. Cook the moussaka, uncovered, for 45 minutes or until a skewer inserted into the center of the casserole is hot to the touch when withdrawn and the top is browned.

Tomatoes Stuffed with Ground Meat

4 large even-sized tomatoes
¼ cup ground cooked lamb or beef
3 tablespoons butter
1 small onion, finely chopped
2 tablespoons breadcrumbs
1 tablespoon ketchup
pinch each of dried rosemary and marjoram
1 tablespoon leftover gravy from the meat
2 slices of toast, buttered

Method

Set the oven at 375°F. Slice the flower (not stalk) end from the tomatoes and reserve the slices for replacing later.

Use a grapefruit knife to scoop out the seeds and flesh from the tomatoes.

Put the meat in a bowl. Heat the butter in a saucepan and stir in the onion, breadcrumbs, ketchup, rosemary and marjoram, and gravy. Add the contents of the pan to the meat and stir with your hand.

Fill the tomatoes with the meat mixture. Remove the crusts from the toast and halve each piece. Set the toast in a small ovenproof dish and put a tomato on each piece. Cover the tomatoes loosely with buttered foil and bake in the preheated oven for 15 minutes or until a skewer inserted into the center of the tomatoes is hot to the touch when withdrawn.

Replace the reserved tomato slices on a slant and serve at once.

FOR SOPHISTICATED TASTES

This menu offers a lovely variety of dishes and an alternate choice for each course, so you should find some combination to appeal to the occasion. For the first course you can either serve flaked halibut arranged in shells and coated with a pimiento-flavored mayonnaise or offer fillets of sole with a grapefruit garnish and Hollandaise. Follow either one with a ham and chicken mold coated with Madeira sauce, or a boned loin of lamb with a pasta and tomato garnish.

For dessert, we offer an almond-flavored rolled sponge cake with a blackberry and apple sauce for serving, or pass a fresh strawberry sauce and garnish the roll with strawberries as well. Use the timetable on page 100 to help you plan your time in the kitchen.

A red wine is our consultant's choice for this meal; either a Barbera d'Asti (Italian) or Barbera (Californian) would be suitable for serving with either main course. If, however, you would like to serve a white wine with the fish course, then choose an Alsatian or Californian Sylvaner Riesling.

TIMETABLE

Day before
Make either blackberry or strawberry sauce for the dessert.
Prepare stock for lamb; prepare tomato sauce for spaghetti (if serving).
Prepare mayonnaise sauce for cold fish appetizer (if serving).

Morning of party
Poach fish and prepare bell pepper garnish for cold fish appetizer (if serving); *or prepare grapefruit for hot fish appetizer.*
Prepare chicken and ham mold and leave in dish ready for baking (if serving).
Prepare green beans or celery (if serving).
Prepare sauce for chicken and ham mold (if serving).
Make and bake biscuit roulé and refrigerate until serving.

Order of Work

6:45
Preheat the oven to 350°F. (for mold) or 400°F (for lamb).

7:00
Put chicken mold in oven to cook: reheat sauce and keep warm. *Prepare hollandaise (if serving) and keep warm;* or finish cold fish appetizer and refrigerate until serving.

7:15
Put lamb in oven to roast; boil spaghetti and toss with sauce and keep warm. Prepare mushrooms for cooking.

7:45
Put fish in oven to poach (if serving hot appetizer).

8:00
Make sauce for lamb. Serve first course.
Assemble lamb dish just before serving.

Appetizer

Coquilles de Poisson Cordon Bleu

1½ lb fillet of firm white fish (tile, halibut, haddock, cod)
1¼ cups court bouillon
3 large ripe tomatoes
1 red bell pepper (to decorate)

For sauce
1¼ cups thick mayonnaise
1 clove of garlic, crushed with a little salt
1 teaspoon tomato paste
salt and pepper

4 deep scallop shells or individual gratin dishes

Method

Place the fish in a pan, cover with the court bouillon and bring very slowly to the boiling point. Cover with the lid and cook the fish so the liquid is barely bubbling, for 20 minutes or until it is firm and white. Leave the fish in the liquid to cool.

When cold, lift the fish from the court bouillon and remove any skin and bones. With your fingers, break the fish apart into large flakes.

Scald, skin and quarter the tomatoes. Scoop out the seeds into a strainer set over a bowl and reserve the juice. Cut the tomato quarters into thick strips. Core the red pepper and remove the seeds. Slice the pepper into 4 thin rounds.

Whisk the mayonnaise and add the garlic and tomato paste. Taste for seasoning and add salt and pepper with enough of the reserved tomato juice to make a sauce that just falls from the spoon.

Divide the fish and tomatoes among the shells or dishes and coat them with the mayonnaise. Garnish each one with a ring of red pepper and refrigerate until serving.

Court bouillon
Slice 1 large carrot and 1 onion. Place these in a pan with 5 cups of water, bouquet garni, 6 peppercorns, 2 tablespoons vinegar (or the juice of ½ lemon). Salt lightly, cover and simmer 8–10 minutes. Cool and strain.

A taste of sophistication

For Coquilles de Poisson Cordon Bleu, each scallop is served in its shell and garnished with a ring of pimiento. The mayonnaise which coats the scallops is flavored with garlic and tomatoes

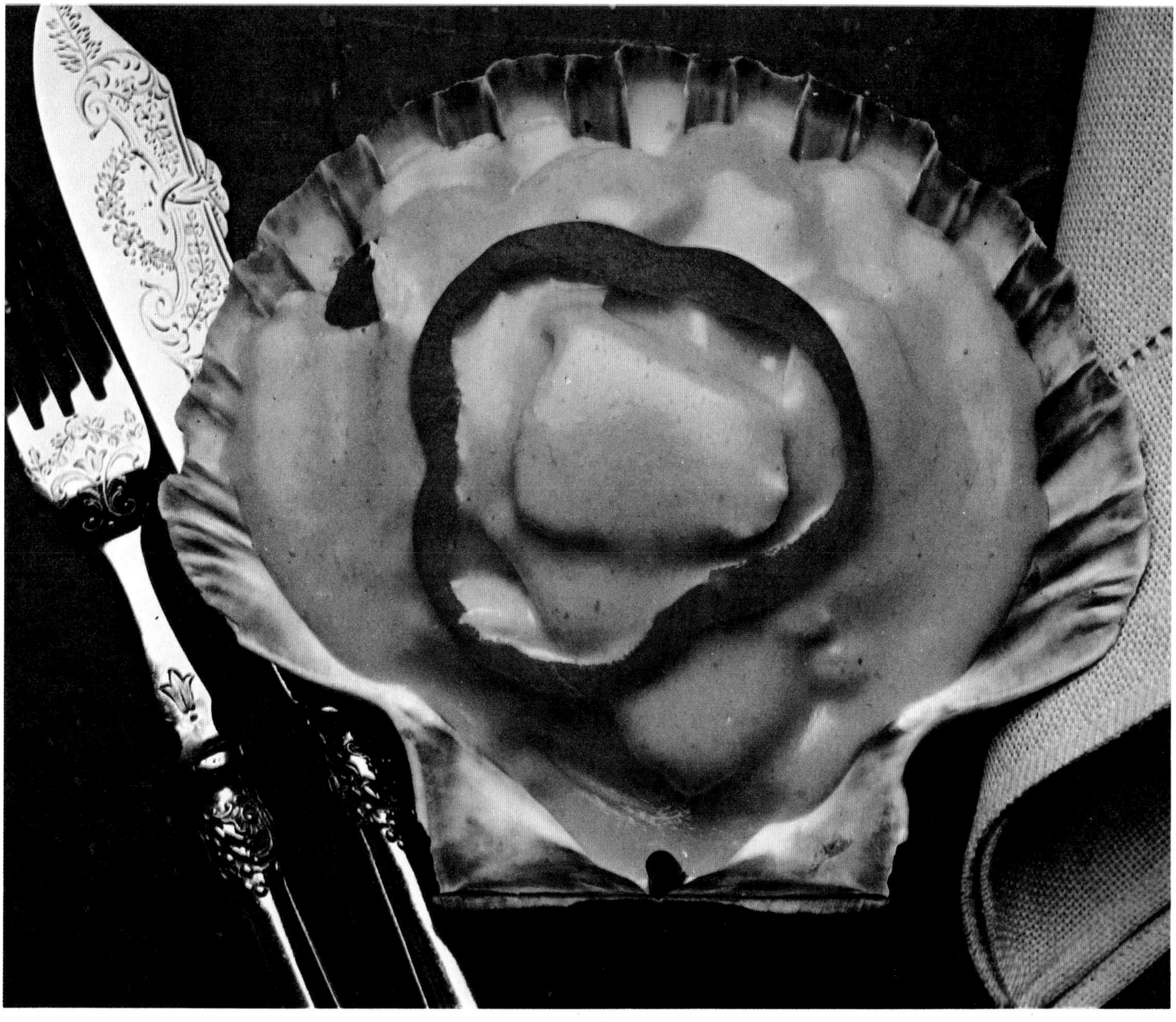

The alternative appetizer for this menu is Filets de Sole Florida; the creamy hollandaise sauce is spooned over each portion just before serving

Alternative appetizer

Filets de Sole Florida

6 fillets of sole
$1\frac{1}{4}$ cups cold court bouillon (see page 100)
2 grapefruit

For hollandaise sauce
$\frac{1}{3}$ cup butter, at room temperature
4 yolks
$1\frac{1}{2}$ tablespoons lemon juice
pinch cayenne pepper
pinch of salt

Method

Set the oven at 325°F. Lightly butter a gratin dish.

Place the unfolded fillets in the gratin dish and cover with the cold court bouillon. Set aside.

Remove the rind and pith from the grapefruits with a serrated-edged knife and slice down between the membranes to make neat sections. Arrange the grapefruit sections down the length of the dish right on the fish.

Cover the dish with buttered foil and set it in the preheated oven. Poach the fish for 15 minutes or until they are white and firm to the touch.

For the hollandaise sauce: put the butter in a small saucepan and heat it just until it has melted, but do not let it brown.

Put the egg yolks, lemon juice, cayenne and a pinch of salt in the container of an electric blender and work at high speed for 15 seconds. Turn down the speed of the blender and remove the insert in the cover. Pour the hot butter into the blender in a thin steady stream; cover and blend for another 5 seconds.

To serve: carefully tip the court bouillon from the baking dish (freeze it and reserve for another fish dish) and transfer the hollandaise to a sauce boat. If you prefer the hollandaise a little thinner, add a teaspoon or two of the court bouillon. Pour the hollandaise over each serving of fish just before passing.

Entrée

Pain de Jambon et Volaille

4 lb roasting chicken
$1\frac{1}{2}$ lb cooked ham
salt and pepper
3 eggs, beaten to mix
$\frac{1}{2}$ cup heavy cream

For panade
4 tablespoons butter
4 tablespoons flour
$1\frac{1}{4}$ cups well-flavored stock
salt and pepper

For sauce madère
3 tablespoons tomato paste
$2\frac{1}{2}$ cups demi-glace sauce (see Vol 21, page 21)
$\frac{1}{3}$ cup Madeira
$1\frac{1}{2}$ tablespoons butter

Soufflé dish (7-cup capacity)

Method

Remove the skin from the chicken and, using a small knife with short sharp strokes, cut every bit of flesh from the carcass. Work the chicken and ham through a grinder into a bowl. Set the oven at 350°F.

(Use the chicken carcass to prepare the $1\frac{1}{4}$ cups well-flavored stock needed for the panade.)

Place the Pain de jambon et volaille in a bain marie for cooking. The sauce madère is shown at side

For the panade: melt the butter in a saucepan, stir in the flour and cook for 2 minutes or until the flour turns straw-colored. Whisk in the stock with salt and pepper to taste and when it is smooth, turn it out onto a plate to cool.

Beat the cooled panade into the ground meats and add plenty of salt and pepper to taste. Beat in the eggs, one by one, followed by the cream.

Butter the soufflé dish, line the bottom with a disc of waxed paper and butter the paper. Turn the mixture into it. Smooth the top, cover with buttered foil and set in a roasting pan.

Pour boiling water around the soufflé dish and set the pan in the oven. Cook for 2 hours, or until a skewer inserted into the mold is hot to the touch when withdrawn. Leave the dish in the roasting pan if necessary to keep it waiting.

For the sauce madère: add the tomato paste to the demi-glace sauce and bring to a boil. Skim the surface and let the sauce simmer until well reduced and concentrated in flavor. Add the Madeira and beat in the butter.

Turn the chicken mold out onto a warm platter and spoon some madeira sauce over the top; pass the remaining sauce separately. Serve with green beans and a julienne of celery.

Alternative entrée

Noisettes d'Agneau Napolitana

2½ lb loin of lamb, completely boned (but reserve bones for stock)
salt and pepper
1 tablespoon chopped mixed herbs (rosemary, marjoram, chives)
4 tablespoons butter
½ cup white wine
½ cup stock
½ lb spaghetti
¼ lb mushrooms
large squeeze of lemon juice

To finish sauce
2 tablespoons sherry
1¼ cups stock (made with lamb bones, 1 sliced onion, 1 sliced carrot, 1 sliced celery stalk, few peppercorns, bouquet garni, 1½ cups water)
2 teaspoons arrowroot mixed with 1 tablespoon water
⅛ lb boiled ham, shredded

For spaghetti sauce
2 lb ripe tomatoes
1½ tablespoons butter
1 onion, finely chopped
1 clove of garlic, crushed
1 tablespoon flour
¾ cup stock
1 tablespoon tomato paste
1 bay leaf

Method

Set the oven at 400°F. Lay the loin on a table, fat side down and sprinkle the inside with salt and pepper, dust with the mixed herbs and roll it tightly. Tie the loin at 2-inch intervals with fine string. Rub the outside with 2 tablespoons of the butter and set the loin in a roasting pan. Pour around the wine and stock and roast the meat in the preheated oven for 1 hour. Baste the meat occasionally during cooking.

Meanwhile, cook the spaghetti in plenty of boiling salted water for 8 minutes, or until al dente. Drain, rinse, and return to the pan with enough hand hot water to cover the pasta; set aside.

Put the mushrooms in a small saucepan with the lemon juice and salt and pepper and cook them over a low heat for 30 seconds. Then cover the saucepan and shake the pan over a high heat for a minute, or until the mushrooms are moist from their own juices.

For the spaghetti sauce: scald and peel the tomatoes and cut them in half through their equators. Squeeze both halves into a strainer set over a bowl so the seeds fall out. Coarsely chop the tomatoes and set aside.

Melt the butter and cook the onion until soft but not brown. Blend in the garlic and flour and cook for 2 minutes or until the flour turns a pale straw-color. Add the tomato flesh, juice from the seeds, stock and tomato paste and bring to a boil, stirring all the time. Add the bay leaf and simmer for 15 minutes or until the sauce is pulpy. Remove the bay leaf and taste for seasoning.

Drain the spaghetti and add 1 tablespoon of the butter to it in a saucepan. Stir in the tomato sauce and keep hot.

To finish the lamb: tip the fat from the roasting pan, leaving the sediment behind. Add the sherry and the stock from the lamb bones and bring to a boil, stirring. Strain into a saucepan.

Stir the arrowroot paste with the remaining 1 tablespoon butter into the sauce and taste for seasoning. Add the shredded ham and keep warm.

Cut the lamb into thick slices ('noisettes') and arrange them around a large platter with mushrooms between each slice. Spoon over enough gravy to moisten them and serve the rest in a sauce boat. Pile the spaghetti in the middle of the platter and serve at once.

A taste of sophistication

Noisettes of lamb are coated with a dark sauce and served with spaghetti tossed in tomato sauce

Biscuit Roulé aux Amandes

$\frac{2}{3}$ cup flour
1 tablespoon cornstarch
$1\frac{1}{2}$ teaspoons baking powder
1 cup sugar
4 eggs, separated
pinch of salt
1 tablespoon cold water
1 teaspoon orange flower water
confectioners' sugar (for sprinkling)

For filling
$1\frac{1}{2}$ cups blanched almonds
$\frac{1}{3}$ cup sugar
3 egg whites
grated rind and juice of 1 lemon
1 cup heavy cream

Jelly roll pan (11 x 16 inches) or paper case

Method

Set the oven at 350°F. Grease the jelly roll pan or paper case. Line the jelly roll pan with waxed paper and grease the paper. Dust the pan or case with flour, tapping out the excess.

Sift together the flour, cornstarch and baking powder four times. Sift the sugar also.

Beat the egg whites with the pinch of salt until they hold stiff peaks. Whisk 3 tablespoons of the sugar into the whites and continue beating for 30 seconds, then fold in 1 more tablespoon sugar.

Put the yolks, water and orange flower water in a bowl and whisk until they start to thicken. Whisk in the remaining sugar a little at a time and continue beating until the mixture leaves a ribbon trail on itself when the beaters are lifted. Fold the whites into the yolks, followed by the flour. Pour the batter into the prepared pan and smooth the top. Bake for 15 minutes or until the top springs back when lightly pressed with a fingertip.

Sprinkle a large sheet of waxed paper or kitchen towel with some granulated sugar and turn jelly roll out onto it. Lift off pan and tear away the paper. Roll up the cake with a sheet of parchment paper or a clean towel on the inside.

For the filling: grind the nuts, then pound them with the sugar, using a mortar and pestle, or work them in a blender a little at a time. Add the egg whites by degrees, adding only enough to make the mixture creamy and not too soft. Add the lemon rind and juice.

Beat the heavy cream until it holds a soft shape and fold it into the almond mixture. Unroll the cooled sponge cake and spread it with the almond cream. Reroll it and slide it onto a platter. Dredge the top with confectioners' sugar and serve with a fruit sauce.

Fresh Strawberry Sauce

1 quart fresh strawberries, hulled
$\frac{3}{4}$ cup water
$\frac{1}{4}$ cup confectioners' sugar, or to taste
2 tablespoons kirsch

Method

Halve the strawberries and put them into a saucepan with the water and the sugar. Bring to a boil, lower the heat and cook gently for 15 minutes, or until the berries are very tender.

Work the strawberries with the liquid in a blender until smooth and add the kirsch. Taste for sweetness and pour into a bowl. If you prefer the sauce a little thinner, add water to dilute it and adjust the sugar again. Chill before serving with biscuit roulé aux amandes, garnished with additional fresh strawberries.

Right: turn the cooked sponge cake onto waxed paper or a kitchen towel and quickly peel off the paper case. Roll up the sponge cake immediately.

Left: spread the cooled sponge cake with the almond-flavored whipped cream and roll up again as shown.

Blackberry and Apple Sauce

1 small cooking apple
1 pint fresh blackberries or 1 can (1 lb) blackberries in syrup
3 tablespoons sugar (if using fresh blackberries)
$1\frac{1}{2}$ teaspoons arrowroot mixed with 1 tablespoon water

Method
Peel and quarter the apple and remove all the core. Slice the apple into a saucepan and add the blackberries. If using fresh berries, add the sugar also. Cover and cook over a low heat for 4 to 5 minutes; (if using fresh berries, add $\frac{3}{4}$ cup water) and continue cooking another 10 minutes or until the berries and apples are both very tender.

Work the mixture through a strainer into a clean pan and taste for sweetness. Return to the boil, whisk in the arrowroot paste and pour into a bowl. Leave until completely cool, then chill before serving with the rolled sponge cake.

The finished cream-filled roll is shown here served with the Blackberry and apple sauce

Chilled lettuce soup is followed by Scallops Celeste and our theater supper ends with Orange dreams

THEATER SUPPER FOR SIX

A white wine would be the one to serve with any of the scallop dishes, and we recommend a beautifully dry Chablis Grand Cru for a special party. A Chardonnay from California would also 'drink well' with this menu.

Dinner before the theater, especially if you're going on a week night, is usually so rushed that the people who have come together to spend an evening are not at all relaxed for the first part of it.

The following supper of chilled lettuce or sour cream soup, scallops in shells and filled oranges can be served partially before the play so you can return later for dessert, or you can have just the first course while the scallops wait for their reheating later (we have given a choice of three scallop dishes). Juggle it as you see what you have time for, and don't let the fact that you're going off to see a good play keep you from enjoying a good meal as well.

Appetizer

Chilled Lettuce Soup

1 full head of romaine lettuce
1 tablespoon butter
1 bunch spring onions (scallions), trimmed and sliced
2 cups chicken stock
salt and pepper
$1\frac{1}{2}$ cups light cream
pinch of grated nutmeg
2 egg yolks

Method

Core the lettuce and break off all the leaves. Wash them thoroughly.

Melt the butter in a saucepan and sauté the spring onions – reserving a few dark green slices – until soft but not brown.

Reserve two of the very small inside leaves of the lettuce for garnish and cut across the remaining leaves in several places to make them easier to handle.

Add the lettuce to the pan with the chicken stock and salt and pepper to taste and bring to a boil. Simmer for 5 minutes.

Leave the soup to cool for an hour, then work it a little at a time in a blender. Pour into a clean saucepan and stir in all but $\frac{1}{2}$ cup of the light cream. Bring to a boil and taste for seasoning; add the grated nutmeg.

Beat the egg yolks with the remaining cream and add a little of the hot soup to them. Stir that into the remaining soup and cook, stirring, until the mixture thickens, but do not let it boil.

Pour the soup into a tureen and leave to cool completely. Just before serving, shred the reserved lettuce leaves and add them to the soup with the scallions for garnish.

TIMETABLE

1 Prepare the soup the day before, then leave in soup tureen in refrigerator; have garnish ready.
2 Prepare and cook scallop mixture and pipe potato purée around shells. Fill the shells a couple of hours before serving and leave on a tray for reheating. *Prepare smetana if serving.*
3 Wash and tear or cut greens for salad and keep in a plastic bag; make dressing and store in a jar.
4 Prepare oranges and fill them, if possible, the afternoon of serving, otherwise before you leave for the theater. Leave on a round platter in the refrigerator ready for their garnish.

Alternative Appetizer

Smetana

2 cups plain yogurt
2 cups sour cream
1 large cucumber
1 bunch spring onions (scallions)
4 tomatoes, peeled, halved and seeded
salt and pepper

Method

Whisk the yogurt and sour cream together. Peel the cucumber and halve it lengthwise. Scoop out the seeds and chop the flesh very finely. Sprinkle with salt and pile into a colander; leave for 20 minutes to drain. Trim and slice the spring onions, reserving a few of the dark slices for garnish.

Cut the tomatoes into shreds and add them to the sour cream mixture with the cucumber, scallions and salt and pepper to taste.

Spoon the mixture into bowls and garnish with the reserved scallions. Refrigerate until serving with pumpernickel bread and butter.

Entreé

Scallops Celeste

2 lb sea scallops
$2\frac{1}{2}$ cups milk
slice of lemon
1 bay leaf
6 peppercorns
3 medium potatoes, peeled and left in cold water
6 tablespoons butter
4 tablespoons flour
$1\frac{1}{2}$ cups grated sharp Cheddar cheese
2 tablespoons fresh white breadcrumbs
sprigs of parsley (for garnish)

6 deep scallop shells; pastry bag and star tip

Method

Put the scallops into a skillet with the milk, lemon, bay leaf, and peppercorns. Bring very slowly to the boil (just when the first bubbles appear at the edges) and remove from the heat. Cover with the lid and leave for 10 minutes, turning the scallops over in the pan after 5 minutes.

Lift out the scallops and strain the milk.

Quarter the potatoes and put them into a saucepan with water to cover. Bring to a boil and simmer for 15 minutes or until they are tender. Drain and return the potatoes to the saucepan and cook over a low heat for a minute to dry them out. Work them through a food mill into a bowl and beat in $\frac{1}{4}$ cup of the strained milk, or enough to give the potatoes a piping consistency. Beat in 2 tablespoons of the butter with plenty of salt and pepper to taste.

Pipe borders all around each scallop shell using the pastry bag fitted with the star tip. Set aside. Set the oven at 425°F.

Melt the remaining 4 tablespoons butter in a saucepan and stir in the flour. Cook 2 minutes, whisking, until the flour starts to turn a pale straw-color, then pour in the remaining milk and whisk constantly until it comes to a boil. Simmer 2 minutes, then take from the heat. Add 1 cup of the cheese and salt and pepper to taste.

Divide the scallops among the shells and coat them with the sauce. Sprinkle the cheese on top of each shell. Dust with the breadcrumbs.

Set the shells on a baking sheet and bake the scallops for 10 minutes or until they are bubbling at the sides and golden brown on top. Garnish with parsley and serve at once.

Alternative entrée 1

Coquilles St. Jacques aux Champignons

2 lb bay or sea scallops
juice of $\frac{1}{2}$ lemon
6 peppercorns
slice of onion
$\frac{1}{2}$ cup water
$\frac{1}{4}$ lb mushrooms
2 tablespoons butter

For sauce
3 tablespoons butter
2 tablespoons flour
$1\frac{1}{2}$ cups milk
salt and pepper
$\frac{3}{4}$ cup grated cheese

6 deep scallop shells

Method
Put the scallops in a large skillet with the lemon juice, peppercorns, onion and the water. Bring very slowly to the boil, turn the scallops in the pan, cover with the lid and remove from the heat.

Cut the mushrooms into thick slices and sauté them briskly over a high heat in the butter. Set the oven at 425°F.

Divide the mushrooms among the scallop shells. Lift the scallops from the pan and divide them among the shells also, discarding any of the seasonings in the liquid. Let the liquid reduce by half.

For the sauce: melt the butter in a saucepan and stir in the flour. Cook for 1 minute, then add the milk and whisk until the mixture comes to a boil. Strain in the reduced scallop cooking liquid and add salt and pepper to taste. Take the sauce from the heat and add all the $\frac{1}{4}$ cup of the cheese. Spoon the sauce over the scallops and sprinkle each one with some of the reserved cheese.

Set the shells on one large baking sheet and cook for 10 minutes or until the sauce is bubbling at the edges and the tops are browned.

Alternative entrée 2

Scallops Hongroises

2 lb bay or sea scallops
$\frac{1}{4}$ lb mushrooms
$1\frac{1}{4}$ cups béchamel sauce (made with 2 tablespoons butter, 2 tablespoons flour, $1\frac{1}{4}$ cups milk)
2 tablespoons butter
salt and pepper
$\frac{1}{2}$ teaspoon paprika
1 tablespoon brandy
$\frac{3}{4}$ cup heavy cream
paprika (for sprinkling)

Method
If using sea scallops, halve them to make two thin discs. Use the bay scallops as is. Halve the mushrooms.

Prepare the béchamel sauce and set aside. Heat the butter in a skillet and sauté the scallops over a high heat, shaking the pan constantly, for 3 minutes. Add salt and pepper to taste. Put the mushrooms in the pan and continue to cook for another minute or two or until the mushrooms are just tender. Sprinkle in the paprika and stir well. Pour in the brandy and let it reduce completely. Add the béchamel sauce and let the contents of the pan come to the boiling point. Add the cream and taste for seasoning. Return to the boil and tip into a serving dish. Sprinkle the top with a little more paprika and serve at once.

Dessert

Orange Dreams

6 navel oranges
1 juice orange
1 envelope unflavored gelatin
1 cup heavy cream
2 tablespoons Grand Marnier or other orange-flavored liqueur
6 bay leaves (for garnish)

Method
Wipe the oranges and slice off the navel end by making small 'v' shapes all the way around. Cut a very thin slice from the other end so the open oranges sit firmly in place.

Scoop out the insides of the oranges with a serrated-edged knife and pile them in a strainer set over a bowl. Grate the rind from the juice orange and juice it into the strainer.

Sprinkle the gelatin over the orange juice and leave for 5 minutes to sponge. Then dissolve the gelatin over a pan of hot water.

Whip the cream until it holds a soft shape, then pour in the orange juice, orange rind and orange liqueur. Stir the cream over a bowl filled with ice until it is on the point of setting.

Fill the oranges with a spoon, or with a pastry bag fitted with a large plain round tip. Refrigerate until serving, then garnish each one with a bay leaf just before taking them to the table.

Potage crème Hawaii with Savory mille feuilles, Sugared ham and Spiced peaches; for dessert — an Orange and almond gâteau

BUFFET SUPPER FOR TWELVE

Potage Crème Hawaii

Savory Mille Feuilles
Spiced Peaches
Sugared Ham

Mexican Salad
Fennel and Cabbage Salad

Orange and Almond Gâteau

White wine – Niersteiner (Rheinhessen)
or Johannisberg Riesling (California)

The most efficient way to serve a dozen guests is buffet-style, with an appetizer that you can pass first on a tray or set on the table with the remaining dishes. The chicken and puff pastry entrée, assembled as a mille feuilles, makes a very special dish and the accompanying salads offer exciting color and texture to go with it. Dessert is a multi-layered moka-flavored cake sandwiched with an almond butter filling and glazed with a coffee icing.

Though the main course – the savory mille feuilles is very rich, we would serve a full-bodied Niersteiner – white wine from the Rheinhessen district of Germany – or a Californian Johannisberg Riesling – with this party menu.

Potage Crème Hawaii

2 small pineapples
6 cups well-flavored stock
3 tablespoons butter
3 tablespoons flour
3 egg yolks
1 cup light cream
salt and pepper
2 tablespoons freshly snipped chives

Method

Peel the pineapple and cut out the core. Set the flesh aside.

Slice the cores thinly and add it to the stock in a saucepan. Bring to a boil, take from the heat and cover with the lid. Leave the pineapple in the stock for 30 minutes to infuse. Strain.

Shred the pineapple flesh; pile into a bowl and refrigerate.

Melt the butter in a large saucepan and stir in the flour. Cook 2 minutes or until the flour begins to turn a pale straw-color, then whisk in the stock and bring to a boil, stirring. Simmer for 5 minutes.

Whisk the egg yolks with the light cream and add several spoonfuls of the soup to it. Stir that back into the remaining soup and cook over a gentle heat until the soup thickens slightly, but do not let it boil or it will curdle.

Chill the soup until it is completely cold, then stir in the shredded pineapple and taste for seasoning. Pour into a chilled soup tureen. Garnish the top with the fresh chives and ladle into bowls or cups for serving.

Savory Mille Feuilles

4 cup quantity puff pastry (see Volume 15, page 19)
2 tablespoons freshly grated Parmesan cheese

For filling
4 lb roasting chicken
1 onion, halved
1 carrot, halved
1 stalk celery, quartered
bouquet garni
béchamel sauce (made with 4 tablespoons butter, 4 tablespoons flour, 2 cups infused milk)
salt and pepper
1 envelope unflavored gelatin sprinkled over 2 tablespoons chicken stock

For liver mixture
1 cup butter, at room temperature
1 lb chicken livers
1 onion, finely chopped
1 clove of garlic, chopped

Method

Set the oven at 425°F. Roll out the pastry and cut it into six 12 x 4-inch strips. Prick well all over and place on a dampened baking sheet. Chill 10 minutes, then dust two strips with the grated Parmesan cheese and bake the strips in the preheated oven for 10 minutes or until browned. Take from the oven and set on racks to cool.

Put the chicken in a kettle with the onion, carrot, celery, and bouquet garni and enough water to come up to the breast of the chicken.

Bring to a boil, skim the scum that rises to the surface, cover and cook the chicken for $1\frac{1}{2}$ hours or until tender. Leave in the liquid to cool slightly, then lift out and cool on a plate.

When the chicken is cool enough to handle, skin it and strip the meat from the bones. Work the meat through a grinder into a bowl. Add the béchamel sauce with salt and pepper to taste.

For the liver mixture: melt 2 tablespoons of butter in a large skillet and sauté the livers and onion over a high heat for 5 minutes until the livers are very firm. Add the garlic and continue cooking another 2 minutes. Transfer the livers to a bowl and chill until very cold.

Work the livers through a grinder into a bowl and beat in the remaining butter with plenty of salt and pepper to taste.

Dissolve the gelatin over a bowl of hot water and stir it into the chicken mixture. Stir that mixture over a bowl filled with ice cubes until it is on the point of setting and divide the mixture between two of the plain strips. Smooth with a palette knife. Set two more plain strips on top and spread the liver mixture on them. Cover with the Parmesan-topped strips and set the mille feuilles on one or two large platters and surround with the spiced peaches and sugared ham.

Spiced Peaches

1 can (2 lb) peach halves in syrup
2 tablespoons white wine vinegar
3 sticks cinnamon
6 peppercorns
2 cloves
2 tablespoons light brown sugar

Method

Put the peach halves in their syrup in a saucepan with the vinegar, cinnamon sticks, peppercorns, cloves and light brown sugar. Bring slowly to the boil and stir carefully so the sugar dissolves. Take from the heat and cover. Leave for 10 minutes.

Lift the peaches from the liquid with a slotted spoon and boil the syrup in the pan until it is very thick and reduced by half. Strain it over the peaches and leave to cool completely. Arrange on the platter with the slices of ham.

Sugared Ham

$2\frac{1}{2}$ lb piece cooked ham
$\frac{1}{2}$ cup light brown sugar
handful of whole cloves
$\frac{3}{4}$ cup apple cider

Method

Set the oven at 350°F. Score the fat side of the ham in a lattice pattern and rub it with the brown sugar. Set a clove into the center of each diamond and put the ham in a roasting pan. Pour the cider around it and bake in the preheated oven for 45 minutes or until the sugar is golden brown, basting with the liquid in the pan occasionally during cooking.

Cut into very thin slices and arrange on the mille feuilles platter with the peaches.

Mexican Salad

8 small red potatoes
2 cans (1 lb each) corn kernels
2 red or green peppers, cored, seeded and diced
1 celery heart, trimmed and thinly sliced
salt and pepper
1 cup vinaigrette dressing (made with 4 tablespoons white wine vinegar, salt and pepper, dry mustard, $\frac{3}{4}$ cup oil.

Method

Boil the potatoes in their skins for 15 minutes, or until they are tender. Peel them and cut them into large dice. Pile them into a bowl. Drain the corn and add to the potatoes.

Drop the peppers into a saucepan of boiling water and cook 1 minute; drain and refresh. Add to the bowl of vegetables with the celery, salt and pepper and the vinaigrette dressing. Stir well, cover and chill.

Fennel and Cabbage Salad

Fennel is a white bulbous root which can weigh about 1 pound each. To use it raw, slice it thinly and add it carefully to salads, because of its strong anise taste.

$\frac{1}{2}$ root of fresh fennel
1 large firm white cabbage
about $\frac{3}{4}$ cup oil
$\frac{1}{4}$ cup white wine vinegar
salt and pepper
handful fresh parsley, finely chopped

Method

Slice the fennel as thinly as possible and pile it into a large bowl. Quarter and core the cabbage and cut each section as thinly as possible, adding the cabbage shreds to the bowl of fennel.

Add the oil slowly, turning the vegetables constantly so they all become coated with it. Sprinkle with the vinegar and salt and pepper to taste and keep turning. Add the parsley, taste for seasoning and pile into a serving dish. Chill thoroughly before serving.

Orange and Almond Gâteau

$\frac{3}{4}$ cup whole blanched almonds
4 eggs
1 cup sugar
1 cup flour
pinch of salt
1 tablespoon dry instant coffee dissolved in 1 tablespoon hot water

For filling
6 tablespoons butter
$\frac{2}{3}$ cup sugar
$\frac{3}{4}$ cup finely chopped almonds
$\frac{2}{3}$ cup heavy cream
2 tablespoons chopped candied orange peel

For apricot glaze
$\frac{1}{2}$ cup apricot jam
juice of $\frac{1}{2}$ orange

For glacé icing
$1\frac{1}{2}$ cups confectioners' sugar, sifted
1 teaspoon dry instant coffee dissolved in 1 tablespoon hot water
1 tablespoon apricot jam glaze

8-inch springform pan

Method

Set the oven at 350°F. Grease the springform pan, dust it with sugar and tap out the excess. Grind the almonds.

Beat the eggs and sugar until very thick and mousse-like. The mixture should leave a ribbon trail when the beaters are lifted. The pan of hot water helps speed things up when a hand beater is used

Put the almonds onto a baking sheet and cook them in the oven for 12 minutes or until lightly toasted. Leave to cool.

Beat the eggs and sugar until very thick and mousse-like and the mixture leaves a ribbon trail on itself when the beaters are lifted. Use an electric mixer on high speed or set a bowl over a pan of steaming hot water and use a rotary beater.

Sift the flour with the salt and fold $\frac{2}{3}$ of the flour into the mousse mixture. Add the coffee and almonds and fold lightly, then fold in the remaining flour. Turn the mixture into the prepared pan and smooth it so it is slightly higher in the center.

Bake in the preheated oven for 1 hour or until the cake springs back when lightly pressed with a fingertip. Leave to cool in the pan.

For the filling: melt the butter, add the sugar and bring to a boil. Add the nuts, and cook the mixture to a biscuit color. Pour in the cream, return to a boil, and simmer gently for 2 minutes, or until thick. Add the candied peel and pour into a bowl to cool completely.

Cut the cake into thirds and sandwich them with the cooled filling.

For the apricot glaze: heat the jam with the orange juice and bring to a boil. Simmer 2 minutes, then brush on the cake in a fairly thin layer.

For the glacé icing: mix the confectioners' sugar with the coffee. Add the apricot glaze and warm the icing over a bowl of hot water until it is glossy and shiny. Leave to cool slightly, then pour over the cake to glaze it.

Lift the cake onto a round platter and leave for several hours before serving.

Start with Lobster bouchées (center), then there's a Galantine of chicken and tongue (bottom left) or Ham roulades (behind it) and a choice of salads. There's a Corn and potato salad (left rear) and a Summer salad (right front). For dessert, try Brown sugar meringues with a fruit salad, or offer a freezer cake – Pavé au chocolat, decorated with whipped cream and flavored with brandy

A RECEPTION FOR TWENTY-FOUR

People who cook all the time say it takes just as much work to prepare a dinner party for eight guests as it does to cook for two dozen. In fact, the larger number is often easier in the end because all the food being served is presented at the same time and the guests are left to help themselves. Vary the hot and cold foods so you don't find yourself short of oven space and use your freezer to store pastry in large batches so you'll have it already made when the time comes. The galantine (without the glaze) and gratin de légumes can be made ahead of time and frozen. The pavé au chocolat, however, *must* be frozen for at least a day.

Once again, a white wine is our expert's choice for this summery menu; this time he selects an Alsatian Riesling, or an Emerald Riesling from California, to complement either the ham roulades and summer salad, or the winter-warming, delicate-tasting gratin of vegetables.

Bouchées of Lobster, Salmon or Shrimp

Chicken and Tongue Galantine
Endive, Apple and Celery Salad

Roulades de Jambon
with Sweet Corn, Cucumber and New Potato Salad

Summer Salad
or
Gratin de Légumes

Meringues Créole with Macedoine de Fruits
Pavé au Chocolat

White wine – Riesling (Alsace)
or Emerald Riesling (California)

Bouchées of Lobster, Salmon or Shrimp

2 cup quantity puff pastry (see Vol 8)
1 egg, beaten to mix (for glaze)

For filling
$\frac{1}{2}$ lb salmon steaks, poached in court bouillon (see Vol 21)
or $\frac{1}{2}$ lb lobster meat, boiled until tender
or $\frac{1}{2}$ lb cooked shrimps, halved

For sauce
2 tablespoons butter
$1\frac{1}{2}$ tablespoons flour
1 cup fish stock (see page 00)
salt and pepper
2 tablespoons heavy cream
$\frac{1}{4}$ lb mushrooms, quartered
juice of 1 lemon

$2\frac{1}{2}$-inch fluted pastry cutter; 1-inch plain cutter

Method
Roll out the pastry to a $\frac{1}{4}$-inch thickness and stamp out 16 rounds with the fluted cutter. With the plain cutter, make a mark in the centers of these rounds, cutting down slightly into the dough (but not all the way through). Lift the rounds onto a dampened baking sheet. Brush them with egg glaze, taking care not to let the glaze drip down the sides of the pastry.

Chill the baking sheet for 15 minutes. Meanwhile, set the oven at 425°F.

Bake the bouchées for 15–20 minutes or until they are puffed and golden brown. Lift onto a wire rack to cool. While still warm, lift out the center 'lid' with the point of a knife and scoop out any soft center with a teaspoon. Reserve the lids.

For the sauce: melt the butter in a saucepan and stir in the flour. Cook 2 minutes, stirring, until the flour turns a pale straw-color, then whisk in the fish stock and bring to a boil. Simmer 2 minutes, then add salt and pepper to taste and stir in the heavy cream.

Cook the mushrooms in the lemon juice in a covered saucepan for 2 minutes or until the mushrooms are just tender. Flake the salmon or cut up the lobster meat and add it or the shrimps to the sauce with the mushrooms.

To serve: reheat the pastry cases in a preheated 350°F oven for 10 minutes or until warm. Bring the sauce to a boil again and keep warm in a water bath if necessary. Fill each pastry case with the seafood and arrange them on a platter for serving at once.

Fish Stock
Peel and slice 1 large onion, blanch, drain and refresh it. Melt 1 tablespoon butter in a large saucepan, add the onion and 1 lb washed fish bones, cover and cook slowly for 5 minutes. Add 1 carrot, peeled and sliced, 1 stalk of celery, sliced, 5 cups water, bouquet garni, $\frac{1}{2}$ teaspoon salt, 6 peppercorns, $\frac{1}{2}$ cup dry white wine and a slice of lemon. Simmer gently, uncovered, for 20 minutes; strain and measure.

Stamping rounds from puff pastry: cut the rounds from the rolled pastry, keeping the cuts very close together, but try not to use the pastry all around the edge of the rolled piece so the rounds rise evenly. Puff pastry always shrinks slightly during baking, so expect the $2\frac{1}{2}$-inch rounds to make 2-inch bouchée cases.

Chicken and Tongue Galantine

8 lb capon
$1\frac{1}{2}$ lb tongue in one piece
$\frac{1}{2}$ cup shelled pistachio nuts
1 cup meat glaze (see box)
bunch of watercress (for garnish)

For stuffing
1 onion, finely chopped
2 tablespoons butter
$1\frac{1}{2}$ lb ground veal
1 cup fresh white breadcrumbs
1 egg, beaten to mix
$\frac{3}{4}$ cup heavy cream
salt and pepper

Trussing needle and string

Method

For the stuffing: cook the onion in the butter until soft but not brown. Leave until completely cool. Work the ground veal and breadcrumbs together in a bowl and beat in the cooled onion, egg, cream and plenty of salt and pepper to taste.

Bone the capon starting from the back and split the skin down the length of the backbone. Cut away the meat from the thighs, then the legs, then remove the wings and cut the meat from the carcass all along the breastbone. Spread the skin on the board and distribute the meat evenly on it. Lay the stuffing on the meat.

Cut the tongue into finger-length pieces and lay these down the length of the chicken alternately with some pistachio nuts. Shape the stuffing and chicken into a roll and bring up the edges of the skin over them. Sew up the length of the skin with a trussing needle and string and wrap the galantine in a clean dish towel. Tie the dish towel with string at either end, so it looks like a giant sausage and put a safety pin in two places along the seam so it stays tightly closed.

Bring a large fish poacher or kettle of water to the boil and put in the galantine. Return to the boil, cover and simmer gently for 2 hours or until a skewer inserted into the center of the galantine is hot to the touch when withdrawn. Lift up the galantine and leave until just cool enough to handle. Then untie the kitchen towel and re-tie it so it is very tight once again around the capon.

Refrigerate overnight. Unwrap the roll and carefully cut away the stitches along the skin.

Set the galantine on a wire rack with a tray underneath. Heat the meat glaze to dissolve it and brush the warm glaze over the galantine to coat it completely. Leave to set in the refrigerator for 15 minutes or until firm, then brush again a couple of times.

To serve: cut the first 3 or 4 slices from the galantine and arrange them overlapping at one end of the serving platter. Set the galantine down the center and garnish the platter with watercress.

True meat glaze is made from strained brown stock, boiled down and skimmed constantly, until it is a thick, syrupy brown color. Pour into a container and store in the refrigerator for a month.

Endive, Apple and Celery Salad

6 large heads of endive
3 Courtland apples
1 large head of celery, trimmed

For dressing
grated rind of $\frac{1}{2}$ lemon
juice of 1 lemon
2 tablespoons sugar
6 tablespoons oil
$\frac{2}{3}$ cup heavy cream
salt and pepper
bunch of parsley, finely chopped

Method

Remove the cores from the endive and cut them into thick diagonal slices. Quarter and core the apples and cut each quarter into thin slices. Cut the celery into short bâtons and combine the three vegetables in a large bowl.

Whisk the lemon rind, juice, sugar and oil together and gradually add the heavy cream, whisking steadily. Add salt and pepper to taste and pour over the salad with the parsley. Stir all the ingredients well until thoroughly combined. Pile into a serving dish and chill until ready to put on the buffet.

Roulades de Jambon

12 thin slices of boiled ham
8 oz package cream cheese, at room temperature
salt and pepper
3 tablespoons light cream
$\frac{3}{4}$ cup finely chopped pecans
$\frac{1}{4}$ lb piece Virginia ham, finely chopped

For salad
2 long European cucumbers
salt
1 honeydew melon
3 tomatoes, peeled, halved and seeded
2 tablespoons chopped fresh mint, chives and parsley
$\frac{1}{2}$ cup vinaigrette dressing (made with 2 tablespoons vinegar, salt and pepper, generous $\frac{1}{3}$ cup oil)

Method
Beat the cream cheese until soft and light. Add plenty of salt and pepper to taste and beat in the light cream, chopped nuts and ham. Spread some of this mixture on each slice of boiled ham and roll up. Set on a tray and cover tightly with plastic film.

For the salad: peel the cucumbers and cut them into large cubes. Sprinkle lightly with salt and pile into a colander; leave for 30 minutes to drain, then rinse with cold water and dry on paper towels.

Halve the melon and remove the seeds. Cut each half into half again and cut off the skin. Cut the melon into cubes.

Cut the tomato halves into half again and combine them in a bowl with the cucumber and melon cubes. Pour in the chopped mint, chives and parsley and the vinaigrette dressing and stir carefully with a rubber spatula. Add salt and pepper to taste, cover tightly with plastic film and refrigerate until very cold.

To serve: arrange the roulades in a deep serving dish and cover them with the salad and dressing.

Sweet Corn, Cucumber and New Potato Salad

2 packages (10 oz) each frozen corn kernels
1 cucumber
12 new potatoes
about 1 cup vinaigrette dressing (see previous recipe)
salt and pepper
2 tablespoons chopped parsley

Method
Bring a saucepan of water to the boil, add the corn, return to the boil, and cook only until the corn breaks apart. Drain and rinse with cold water.

Peel the cucumber and halve it lengthwise. Remove the seeds with a teaspoon and cut the flesh into large dice.

Scrub potatoes and drop them into a large pan of boiling salted water. Cook steadily for 12 minutes or until they are tender, then drain and peel them while they are still hot.

Pour enough vinaigrette dressing over the potatoes to moisten them and leave them until completely cool. Add the sweet corn, diced cucumber and remaining dressing and stir well. Season with plenty of salt and pepper to taste and sprinkle with the chopped parsley. Pile into a bowl and chill before serving.

The Summer salad (see recipe at right) is shown with the Ham roulades and their cucumber, melon, and tomato garnish. This makes a good summer menu for this buffet

Summer Salad

6 ripe tomatoes
2 heads of broccoli
1 cup vinaigrette dressing (see recipe for Roulades de Jambon)
1 lb mushrooms
2 tablespoons oil
4 cucumbers
salt and pepper
1 lb green beans, trimmed
1 bunch spring onions (scallions), trimmed and sliced

Method

Scald and peel tomatoes and remove cores. Halve them and squeeze each half over a plate so the seeds pop out. Cut into slices and set aside.

Peel the stems from the broccoli and cut each stalk into 2-inch pieces. Drop them into boiling salted water and cook for 3 minutes or until they are tender but still crisp. Drain and rinse with cold water.

Pile the broccoli into a large bowl with half of the vinaigrette dressing and set aside.

Trim a slice from the stem end of the mushrooms. Heat the oil in a large skillet and sauté the mushrooms over a high heat very quickly. Remove from the pan and pile into the bowl of broccoli.

Peel the cucumber so it is striped and slice thinly; sprinkle the slices with salt and pile them into a colander to drain for 30 minutes. Rinse and pat dry with paper towels.

Cut the green beans into 2-inch pieces and drop them into boiling salted water; return to the boil and continue cooking for 2 minutes or until just done. Drain and refresh.

Arrange the string beans in the bottom of a large dish and sprinkle with the broccoli and mushrooms. Scatter with half the spring onions and add salt and pepper to taste.

Make a circle of cucumber slices all around the edge of the dish and pile the tomato in the center of that border. Arrange the remaining cucumber slices in the center of the tomatoes and pour the remaining vinaigrette dressing over the vegetables. Scatter with the rest of the spring onions and cover tightly. Refrigerate until serving.

The Gratin de légumes is a filling winter alternative

Gratin de Légumes

4 large Spanish onions, thinly sliced
8 tablespoons butter
1 lb carrots, thinly sliced
salt and pepper
1 teaspoon sugar
1 teaspoon chopped fresh mint
1 lb mushrooms
1 large head of cauliflower
3 medium potatoes
1 egg yolk
1 tablespoon heavy cream

For mornay sauce
3 tablespoons butter
3 tablespoons flour
2 cups milk
½ cup grated Cheddar cheese

Pastry bag; star tip

Method

Cook the onions in 3 tablespoons of the butter until soft and golden brown. Put them in the bottom of a 14-inch ovenproof deep dish.

Put the carrots into a saucepan with water to cover, salt and pepper, the sugar and 1 tablespoon of the butter and bring to a boil. Cook steadily until all the water has evaporated, watching the pan closely towards the end of cooking. Toss the carrots with the mint and spoon them onto the onions.

Trim the mushrooms and sauté them quickly in 3 tablespoons of the butter. Add salt and pepper to taste and arrange over the carrots.

Remove the core from the cauliflower and cut it into flowerets. Drop into boiling salted water and cook for 8 minutes or until just tender. Drain and spread over the other vegetables.

Peel and quarter the potatoes and put them into a saucepan with water to cover. Bring to a boil and boil steadily for 15 minutes or until the potatoes are tender. Drain, return to the pan and dry them for 1 minute over a gentle heat, then work them through a food mill into the saucepan and beat in the remaining tablespoon butter with the egg yolk and cream. Add salt and pepper to taste.

For the mornay sauce: melt the butter in a saucepan, stir in the flour and cook for 2 minutes or until the flour is straw-colored. Whisk in the milk and bring to a boil, stirring, until the mixture thickens. Simmer 2 minutes, then add salt and pepper to taste and take from the heat. Stir in the cheese. Spoon the sauce over the vegetables and smooth them with a rubber spatula.

Pile the puréed potatoes into the pastry bag fitted with the star tip and pipe a lattice of potatoes across the top of the baking dish. Make a border all around the edge of the dish.

Set the oven at 400°F.

Just before serving: bake the dish in the preheated oven for 25–30 minutes or until the mixture is bubbling at the edges and browned on the top. Serve at once.

Macédoine de Fruits

3 large oranges
1 fresh pineapple
4 bananas
1 quart fresh strawberries
1 lb seedless green grapes
3 tablespoons kirsch
$\frac{1}{4}$ cup sugar
$\frac{1}{2}$ cup water

Method

Peel the oranges using a serrated-edged knife and working round and round until the skin and pith are completely removed. Then remove the segments by cutting down between each membrane. Pile into a bowl.

Peel the pineapple and cut away the eyes. Cut into thick slices and remove the core from each piece. Cut each thick slice into quarters. Add to the oranges.

Peel the bananas and cut diagonally into thick slices. Add to the bowl of fruits. Remove the stems from the strawberries and add them to the bowl. Take the grapes from their stems and add to the remaining fruits. Sprinkle with 2 tablespoons kirsch and stir carefully.

Heat the sugar with the water over a very gentle heat until the sugar is dissolved. Bring to a boil and boil 2 minutes, then set in a bowl filled with ice and stir until the syrup is cool.

Pour the syrup over the fruits in the bowl and sprinkle in the rest of the kirsch. Turn carefully with a rubber spatula and cover tightly with plastic wrap until ready to serve.

Meringues Créole

6 egg whites
2 cups brownulated sugar

For filling
6 cubes of sugar
1 orange
1$\frac{1}{4}$ cups heavy cream

Two baking sheets lined with parchment paper; pastry bag and $\frac{1}{4}$-inch plain round tip.

Method

Set the oven at 250°F. Beat the whites until they hold stiff peaks, then beat in a tablespoon of the sugar. Fold in the remaining sugar. Pipe the meringues with the plain round tip onto the parchment paper-lined baking sheets. Bake them in the preheated oven for 1 hour or until firm to the touch. After 45 minutes in the oven, gently lift the meringues from the baking sheet and press in the flat side to make a very slight hollow. Return to the oven for the last 15 minutes' cooking.

Take out and leave to cool.

Rub the sugar cubes over the rind of the orange to saturate them with the zest. Squeeze juice from the orange. Crush the cubes with the end of a rolling pin and add enough orange juice to dissolve them. Whip the cream until it holds a soft peak, beat in the orange mixture and continue beating until stiff.

Fill the meringues with the orange-flavored cream, sandwiching two together. Pile on a platter and refrigerate until serving with a macédoine of fruits.

Pavé au Chocolat

For chocolate cookies
1 cup butter, at room temperature
$\frac{2}{3}$ cup sugar
$\frac{1}{2}$ cup sweetened cocoa powder
2 cups flour
$\frac{1}{2}$ teaspoon baking powder

For chocolate cream
6 squares (6 oz) semisweet chocolate
$\frac{1}{3}$ cup strong black coffee
1 cup heavy cream
1 teaspoon rum
$\frac{1}{4}$ cup heavy cream, stiffly whipped (for decorating)
confectioners' sugar (for sprinkling)

Method

For the chocolate cookies: cream the butter until soft and light. Beat in the sugar gradually, then beat in the cocoa powder, flour and baking powder. Chill the dough for 10 minutes.

Set the oven at 350°F.

Divide the mixture into walnut-sized balls and place on ungreased baking sheets. Pat the balls with your palm to flatten them and bake the cookies in the preheated oven for 20–25 minutes or until firm to the touch. Take out, leave to cool for a couple of minutes, then transfer cookies to a rack to cool.

For the chocolate cream: melt the chocolate in a saucepan over a gentle heat with the coffee until thick and smooth. Leave to cool, stirring occasionally, until the chocolate mixture becomes the consistency of thick cream. Whip the 1 cup heavy cream until it holds a soft shape and fold in the chocolate with the rum. Sandwich the chocolate cookies together with the chocolate cream, standing them on their edges and place, wrapped in foil, in the freezer for 1–2 days.

Remove from the freezer and place in the refrigerator, for 1 hour, then decorate the top of the pavé with a ruff of whipped cream and dust the cake with a little confectioners' sugar. Cut the cake on the diagonal into slices.

Front: rich, dark Pavé au chocolat. Behind: Meringues créole sandwiched with orange cream

A magnificent buffet spread greets your guests for a truly special celebration

A GRAND PARTY FOR FIFTY

To finish on a celebratory note, we offer a very special table suitable for a christening party, wedding reception, or other family occasion. The spread includes assorted canapés, tiny tartlets and hot cocktail foods, followed by an assortment of sweets, from the familiar éclairs to more unusual brandy curls. The end result is really rather grand and if you do much of the busy work in advance, the final preparations before your party should not be overwhelming.

This time, for our final celebration, we offer a choice of red or white wines for your guests. Beaujolais Villages would be light yet 'round' enough to enjoy with the savories, or choose a Californian red instead – a Gamay Beaujolais, for example. If some of your guests would prefer a white wine, we would serve a deliciously dry and fragrant Pouilly-Fuissé from the Burgundy region of France, or a Californian Chardonnay – either of which would add just the right touch to your special celebration.

Canapés
Smoked Salmon Pinwheels
Ham and Cream Cheese Pinwheels
Asparagus Canapés
Salami Cornucopias

Savory Tartlets
Cheese Tartlets
Smoked Whitefish Tartlets
Smoked Cods' Roe Tartlets
Caviar Tartlets

Hot Savories
Shrimp and Bacon Fritters
Mushroom Beignets
Cheese and Shrimp Aigrettes
Fried Scallops
Deviled Chicken Livers
with Savory Dips

Desserts
Carolines
Jacquelines
Brandy Curls
Gâteaux Punch
Chocolate Cream Cheese Cupcakes
Fruit Tartlets

Red wine – Beaujolais Villages (Burgundy)
or Gamay Beaujolais (California)
White wine – Pouilly-Fuissé (Burgundy)
or Chardonnay (California)

Smoked Salmon Pinwheels

1 unsliced loaf wholewheat bread
8 tablespoons unsalted butter, at room temperature
$\frac{1}{2}$ lb smoked salmon
black pepper
juice of $\frac{1}{2}$ lemon

Method
Put the bread in the freezer for an hour or until it is just beginning to firm. Then trim the rounded top from the loaf and cut away the crusts from the sides. Slice 8 very thin pieces from the length of the loaf and spread them with butter. Divide the smoked salmon among the slices and sprinkle them with black pepper and lemon juice. Roll up lengthwise into tight rolls and wrap each one in foil. Chill for 2 hours.

Cut each roll into half-inch slices for serving – about 5 slices per roll. Set them on a baking sheet in the fridge, tightly covered with plastic film, until ready to arrange on a platter.

Note: the whole bread can be cut into a dozen thin slices, so if you prefer to make more of these pinwheels with the rest of the loaf, increase the proportions listed above half as much again.

Ham and Cream Cheese Pinwheels

$\frac{1}{3}$ lb boiled ham, thinly sliced
1 8-oz package cream cheese, at room temperature
$\frac{1}{2}$ teaspoon celery salt
buttered slices of wholewheat and white bread

$1\frac{1}{2}$-inch plain round cutter

Method
Spread the slices of ham out on the work surface. Beat the cream cheese until soft and light and beat in the celery salt. Spread some of the cream cheese mixture on each slice of ham and roll them up. Wrap each roll in plastic film and refrigerate for at least 3 hours.

Cut each ham roll into eight even slices with a very sharp knife, wiping the blade after each cut.

Stamp rounds from the bread with the plain cutter and set each pinwheel on a small round. Set the canapés on a tray and cover tightly with plastic film until ready to arrange on a platter.

Asparagus Canapés

1 unsliced loaf of wholewheat bread
6 tablespoons unsalted butter, at room temperature
1 teaspoon Dijon-style mustard
2 lb fresh asparagus
½ can consommé
½ envelope unflavored gelatin

Method

Cut the crusts from the loaf and cut about seven ¼-inch thick slices. Work the butter with the mustard and spread it on the slices of bread. Divide each slice in thirds to make finger lengths and set aside. (You should have as many fingers of bread as you have asparagus spears, so cut more slices from the loaf if necessary.)

Cut the asparagus spears so the tips are 2-inches long and drop them into boiling water. Return to the boil and cook them for 2 minutes or until they are tender but still quite crisp. Drain and refresh.

Set an asparagus spear on each finger of bread and set them all on a rack with a tray underneath.

Put the consommé into a small saucepan and sprinkle over the gelatin. Leave for 5 minutes, then dissolve over a gentle heat, but do not let it boil. Stir the consommé over a bowl filled with ice water until it is on the point of setting.

Spoon a little of the aspic over each piece of asparagus so they are all coated with this glaze. Transfer to a tray and refrigerate until ready to arrange on a platter.

Salami Cornucopias

20 slices of salami
1 8-oz package cream cheese, at room temperature
salt and pepper
1 cap of pimiento, finely chopped
40 small unsalted crackers

Pastry bag and ½-inch plain round tip

Method

Remove any rind from the salami and cut each slice in half. Beat the cream cheese in an electric mixer until it is soft and light. Beat in salt and pepper to taste and fill the pastry bag fitted with the plain tip with the cream cheese mixture. Curl each piece of salami into a cone shape and secure with a toothpick. Pipe some of the cream cheese mixture into each cone, setting them in a jelly roll pan. Stud the top of each cone with a piece of the chopped pimiento and leave the cream cheese to chill and harden for several hours.

Remove the toothpicks from the salami cones and set them on the crackers; arrange with the other canapés on the platters.

Front: Ham and cheese pinwheels, Salami cornucopias and Asparagus canapés; Right: Smoked salmon pinwheels and Caviar tartlets; behind — a selection of desserts.

Cheese Pastry-filled Tartlets

Flavoring pastry with a high proportion of cheese gives you a base for tartlets which tastes every bit as exciting as the filling with which they are combined. Since cheese tends to scorch easily, watch their cooking time carefully and get the tartlet pans off the hot baking sheets as quickly as possible. You can make the following pastry in large quantity and freeze it uncooked until ready to fill.

Cheese Pastry

4 cups flour
1$\frac{1}{3}$ cups butter
2$\frac{2}{3}$ cups finely grated cheese (preferably half Cheddar and half Parmesan)
salt and pepper
pinch of cayenne pepper
3 egg yolks mixed with $\frac{2}{3}$ cup ice water

Makes enough to line 6 dozen tartlet pans (2-inches in diameter).

Method

Sift the flour into a bowl and cut in the butter with a long metal palette knife until the mixture resembles crumbs. Cut in the cheese with the salt, pepper and cayenne and when the mixture is very fine, add the yolks and water. Work the ingredients to form a dough, knead lightly on a floured board and wrap in plastic film. Chill 30 minutes.

Use one-third of the pastry at a time: roll out the dough and stamp out rounds slightly larger than the pan you will use or pinch off small walnut-sized rounds of dough and flatten them right into the tartlet pans with your fingertips. Chill for 1 hour.

Set the oven at 400°F.

Bake the tartlets on a baking sheet for about 12 minutes or until set and just beginning to turn color at the edges. Remove from oven and slide tartlet pans off baking sheet. Remove pastry from tins when cold.

Cheese Tartlets

2 tablespoons butter
2 tablespoons flour
1$\frac{1}{4}$ cups milk
salt and pepper
1$\frac{1}{2}$ cups grated cheese (half Gruyère and half Cheddar)
2 eggs, beaten to mix
paprika (for sprinkling)

Method

Melt the butter in a saucepan and stir in the flour. Cook this mixture for 2 minutes over a gentle heat, then whisk in the milk and bring to a boil, stirring constantly. Add salt and pepper to taste and cook 1 minute. Take from the heat and stir in the cheese, then the eggs, one at a time.

When 24 pastry-lined tartlet pans have baked for 5 minutes (see previous recipe), take from the oven and press in the bottom of the tartlets (which will rise a little during baking). Fill the tartlets with the cheese mixture and return to the oven for 5 minutes or until the mixture is set and lightly browned. Dust with paprika before serving.

Smoked Whitefish Tartlets

$\frac{1}{3}$ lb boneless smoked whitefish
1 3-oz package cream cheese, at room temperature
4 tablespoons butter, at room temperature
1 teaspoon prepared horseradish
salt and pepper
2 small whole dill pickles, thinly sliced

Method

Pound the whitefish with the cream cheese and butter until it is very smooth. Beat in the horseradish with salt and pepper to taste. When the pastry in the tartlet pans is cool, fill the cases with the mixture and set a slice of dill pickle on top of each one. Set on a tray and cover with plastic film. Refrigerate until ready to arrange on a platter for serving.

Smoked Cods' Roe Tartlets

8-oz jar tarama
3 tablespoons fresh white breadcrumbs
3 tablespoons oil
juice of $\frac{1}{2}$ lemon
2 drops Tabasco sauce, to taste
10 black olives, pitted and halved

Pastry bag and $\frac{1}{2}$-inch plain round tip

Method

Soak the breadcrumbs in the oil. Work the cods' roe in a blender until smooth, then work in the soaked breadcrumbs until they are completely incorporated. Add lemon juice and Tabasco to taste and fill the mixture into the pastry bag fitted with the round tip. When the tartlet cases are cooled, pipe the cods' roe mixture into them and top each one with a piece of black olive. Set on a tray and cover with plastic film. Refrigerate until ready to arrange on the canapé platters.

Caviar Tartlets

$\frac{3}{4}$ cup sour cream
1 jar red lumpfish roe
1 jar black lumpfish roe

Method

Fill two dozen of the cooled pastry cases with the sour cream. Top each one with either the red or black caviar and set on a tray. Refrigerate until ready to arrange on the platter.

HOT SAVORIES

Cheese and shrimp aigrettes with scallops, Shrimp and bacon fritters and two Savory dips

Fritter Batter

$1\frac{1}{4}$ cups flour
pinch of salt
$\frac{1}{2}$ envelope dried yeast
$\frac{1}{2}$ cup warm water
1 tablespoon oil
1 egg white

Method
Sift the flour and salt into a bowl. Mix the yeast with a tablespoon of the water and stir it into the flour with the remaining water and oil. Beat well and add enough additional water if necessary to make a mixture with the consistency of a thick cream. Cover and leave in a warm place for 15 minutes. Beat the egg white until stiff and fold into the batter just before using to coat one of the following:

Shrimp and Bacon Fritters

30 large shrimps
10 slices of bacon

Method
Peel each of the shrimps by pulling out the legs along the inside curve and lifting off the shells.

Stretch the bacon by pressing the flat side of the blade of a large chopping knife all along the strips. Cut each one in thirds. Wrap each shrimp in a slice of bacon and secure with toothpicks.

Dip shrimps in the fritter batter and fry in deep fat heated to 375°F (on a deep fat thermometer) until golden brown. Drain on paper towels and remove the toothpicks when cool.

To serve: place the fritters on a baking sheet and reheat in a 450–500°F oven for 7 minutes or until hot and crisp.

Mushroom Beignets

Choose firm unopened button mushrooms and trim a thin slice from the stalk end. Dip each mushroom into the fritter batter and fry in hot deep fat heated to 375°F until golden brown. Drain and reheat as for shrimp fritters above.

Cheese and Shrimp Aigrettes

3-egg quantity of choux pastry
1 cup freshly grated Parmesan cheese
salt and pepper
$\frac{1}{2}$ teaspoon Dijon-style mustard
1 lb small shrimps, shelled
deep fat for frying
$\frac{1}{4}$ cup freshly grated Parmesan cheese (for serving)

Method
Make the choux pastry and beat in the cheese with plenty of salt and pepper and the mustard. Put the mixture out in teaspoonfuls on a wet baking sheet—you should get about 30. Push a shrimp into the center of each mound and make sure that it is completely covered.

Heat the fat to 375°F on a deep fat thermometer and drop in the aigrettes a few at a time. As they begin to swell, raise the heat under the pan very slightly and watch them carefully.

Cook until pale golden and drain on a wire rack.

Dust with the extra Parmesan cheese and serve at once or reheat later in a preheated 500°F oven for 8 minutes or until hot and crisp.

SAVORY DIPS

Base for Dips

$\frac{1}{2}$ teaspoon salt
pepper
1 teaspoon dry mustard
2 teaspoons sugar
1 tablespoon flour
$\frac{1}{3}$ cup white wine vinegar
$\frac{1}{2}$ cup water
2 tablespoons butter
$\frac{3}{4}$ cup light cream

Method
Mix the salt, pepper, mustard, sugar, flour and white wine vinegar in a saucepan until smooth. Add the water and stir over a gentle heat until the mixture comes to a boil. Simmer 2 minutes, then take from the heat and beat in the butter. Pour into a bowl and cover with a piece of buttered waxed paper pressed right onto the surface. When cold, stir in the cream.
Note: This quantity will make one dip, so double the ingredients above to make both dips.

Savory Dip 1

1 recipe base for dips
1 dill pickle, finely chopped
1 tablespoon finely chopped parsley
1 clove of garlic, crushed
1 teaspoon grated onion
1 tablespoon chopped capers
1 tablespoon chopped green olives

Method
Stir all the ingredients with the base and pile into a bowl. Cover tightly with plastic film and refrigerate until serving.

Savory Dip 2

1 recipe base for dips
$\frac{1}{2}$ green pepper, cored, seeded and chopped
4 stalks of celery, trimmed and chopped
1 clove of garlic, crushed
$\frac{1}{4}$ cup chili sauce
1 tablespoon prepared horseradish
3 tablespoons heavy cream

Method
Stir all the ingredients with the base and pile into a bowl. Cover tightly with plastic film and refrigerate until serving.

Fried Scallops

Bay or sea scallops fried in batter are firm and moist on the inside and crisp and golden on the outside. Dip them in the batter, fry, and reheat as directed above. Serve with both the savory dips.

Deviled Chicken Livers

1 cup chicken livers
2 tablespoons butter
1 teaspoon chopped parsley

For marinade
1 teaspoon prepared English mustard
1 teaspoon Dijon-style mustard
2 tablespoons Worcestershire sauce
2 tablespoons ketchup
2 tablespoons oil
1 teaspoon anchovy paste

Method
Whisk the English and Dijon mustards together with the Worcestershire sauce, ketchup, oil and anchovy paste. Put the livers into this marinade and leave for 2 hours in the refrigerator, turning over occasionally.

Heat the butter in a large skillet and sauté the livers over a high heat or until very firm on the outside. Pour in any marinade from the bowl and continue cooking until it is reduced to a thick sticky glaze on the bottom of the pan. Take the livers from the skillet and slice them thickly on the diagonal. Spear with toothpicks and arrange on a platter. Sprinkle with chopped parsley and serve with one of the savory dips.
Note: cocktail hot dogs and small sausages, fried until golden, can accompany the chicken livers.

Desserts

Carolines

3 egg quantity choux pastry (see box)
$1\frac{1}{4}$ cups heavy cream, stiffly whipped
2 tablespoons instant coffee dissolved in a few drops of water
4 squares (4 oz) semisweet chocolate, chopped
2 tablespoons water
1–2 tablespoons sugar syrup
2 cups fondant icing

Pastry bag and $\frac{3}{8}$-inch plain round tip

Makes about 36.

Method
Set the oven at 375°F. Make the choux pastry and fill into the pastry bag fitted with the plain round tip. Pipe small éclairs onto a dampened baking sheet, making each one about 2–$2\frac{1}{4}$-inches long.

Bake the éclairs in the preheated oven for 10–15 minutes or until they are very firm to the touch. Transfer to a wire rack to cool.

Flavor half the whipped cream with half the coffee and pipe this into half the éclairs. Melt the chocolate with the water in a small saucepan, stirring constantly, and then stir over a bowl of cold water until the chocolate mixture is cool but still liquid. Add a teaspoon of the chocolate mixture to the remaining whipped cream and pipe this into the other Carolines.

Add 1 tablespoon of the sugar syrup to half the fondant and dissolve it in a bowl set over hot water.

Flavor the fondant with the remaining coffee and ice the coffee-filled Carolines with this. Add the remaining fondant to the pan and stir it until dissolved. Stir in the remaining chocolate, add the last tablespoon of sugar syrup to dilute it if necessary and use this to coat the chocolate-filled Carolines.

Arrange the Carolines on a serving platter and refrigerate until the party.

Choux pastry
3 egg quantity
3–4 eggs
$\frac{2}{3}$ cup flour
pinch of salt
$\frac{2}{3}$ cup water
$\frac{1}{3}$ cup butter, cut up

Method
Sift the flour with the salt onto a sheet of waxed paper. Put the water and butter into a large saucepan, bring to a boil and when it is bubbling vigorously, shoot in the flour all at once as you take the pan from the heat. Beat slowly until the mixture is smooth and pulls away from the sides of the pan in a ball.

Cool the mixture for 5 minutes, then beat in 3 eggs one at a time, beating very hard between each one. Whisk the 4th egg in a bowl and beat in enough of it to make a choux paste which holds its shape but is not too stiff.

Use as directed.

Jacquelines

2 egg whites
$\frac{3}{4}$ cup brownulated sugar
$\frac{3}{4}$ cup heavy cream, stiffly whipped
1 teaspoon confectioners' sugar

Pastry bag and $\frac{1}{4}$-inch plain round tip; baking sheets lined with parchment

Method
Set the oven at 275°F. Beat the egg whites until they are stiff, beat in 2 teaspoons of the measured sugar and beat for 1 minute. Fold in the remaining sugar and fill the pastry bag fitted with the small round tip with the mixture.

Pipe tiny mounds of the meringue onto the lined baking sheets and bake them in the preheated oven for 35–40 minutes or until they lift easily from the sheet. Then make a slight indentation on the flat side of each one with your finger and return the trays to the oven for another 10 minutes to dry.

Take the meringues from the oven and leave to cool completely. Whisk the cream with the confectioners' sugar and sandwich the tiny meringues with it. Pile onto a platter and refrigerate until serving.

Brandy Curls

$\frac{1}{2}$ cup butter, cut up
$\frac{1}{2}$ cup sugar
$\frac{1}{3}$ cup dark molasses
$\frac{1}{2}$ cup flour
pinch of salt
1 teaspoon ground ginger
1 teaspoon lemon juice
$\frac{1}{2}$ teaspoon vanilla
$1\frac{1}{2}$ cups heavy cream, whipped until stiff and sweetened with 2 teaspoons sugar

12 cream horn molds; pastry bag and large star tip

Method
Set the oven at 325°F. Combine the butter, sugar and molasses in a saucepan and stir over a gentle heat until the butter has melted and the sugar is dissolved.

Leave to cool for 5 minutes.

Sift the flour, salt, and ginger together and stir them into the saucepan with the lemon juice and vanilla.

Grease two baking sheets and drop the mixture in teaspoonfuls at least 4 inches apart onto them. Bake for 7 minutes or until lightly browned and lacy, then remove cookies from the sheet with a sharp knife and immediately curl them around the cream horn molds.

Remove them from the molds the instant they are set and re-use the molds while the cookies are still hot. If the cookies harden, then return the baking sheet to the oven for a minute until they are soft enough to mold again.

Store the cooled cookies in an airtight container.

Just before serving: fill the whipped cream into a pastry bag fitted with the star tip and pipe it into the brandy curls. Arrange on a platter and refrigerate until just before serving.

Gâteaux Punch

This odd-sounding name is an English dessert made by soaking leftover fruit cake with a syrupy chocolate mixture. The very rich dark result is glazed with a white glacé icing.

1 lb fruitcake
8 tablespoons butter
⅓ cup light corn syrup
4 squares (4 oz) semisweet chocolate, cut up
2 tablespoons rum
1 recipe glacé icing

10-inch pie pan with removable base

Method

Butter the pie pan and line it with a circle of waxed paper. Crumble the cake into very tiny pieces in a bowl. Warm the butter, corn syrup and chocolate in a saucepan over gentle heat until the butter and chocolate have melted. Stir in the rum. Add the cake crumbs and stir well.

Press the mixture into the pie pan and smooth it with a metal palette knife. Refrigerate for 24 hours.

Remove the rim from the pan and set the cake on a rack. Pour the glacé icing over the cake and let it set for an hour until it is completely smooth.

Cut the cake into 1-inch triangles, lift them off the base, and arrange on a platter with the other desserts.

Four of the desserts: a platter of brandy curls; on the stand – Gâteau Punch triangles and tiny brown sugar meringues. At right are the miniature éclairs – called Carolines

Chocolate Cream Cheese Cupcakes

For chocolate mixture
1½ cups flour
1 teaspoon baking soda
1 cup sugar
½ teaspoon salt
¼ cup unsweetened cocoa powder
1 cup water
⅓ cup oil
1 tablespoon vinegar
1 teaspoon vanilla

For cream cheese mixture
1 8-oz package cream cheese, at room temperature
1 egg, beaten to mix
⅓ cup sugar
pinch of salt
6-oz package chocolate chips

Two 12-cup muffin pans (2½-inches diameter) lined with paper cups

Method
Set the oven at 350°F.

For the chocolate mixture: Sift the flour and baking soda into a bowl and stir in the sugar, salt and cocoa powder. Whisk in the water, oil, vinegar and vanilla and beat until smooth. Pour some of the chocolate mixture into the bottom of each paper cup; set aside.

For the cream cheese mixture: beat the cream cheese until soft and light, then beat in the egg, sugar and salt until well mixed. Stir in the chocolate chips and divide this mixture among the cups, spooning it right onto the chocolate.

Bake the muffins in the preheated oven for 20–25 minutes or until puffed and cracked and just firm to the touch. Leave to cool in the pans for 15 minutes, then lift out and set on wire racks to cool completely.

Fruit Tartlets

Line tiny tartlet molds with French flan pastry and bake until crisp. Add a spoonful of vanilla-flavored pastry cream and top with a fresh strawberry, slice of banana, slice of kiwi fruit, or several grapes. Coat with apricot glaze and refrigerate until serving. (See the Index for individual recipes.)

Glacé Icing

1½ cups confectioners' sugar
½ teaspoon vanilla
1 tablespoon rum
2–3 tablespoons sugar syrup

Method
Sift confectioners' sugar into a bowl and add the vanilla, rum and 2 tablespoons of the sugar syrup. Mix to a smooth stiff paste and set the bowl over a pan of very hot water. Heat the icing until it is lukewarm and add enough extra sugar syrup to make an icing which just coats the back of a spoon. If it is too thin, add a little more sifted confectioners' sugar.

Use while it is still warm.

Fondant Icing

2 cups sugar
¾ cup water
2 tablespoons corn syrup, or pinch of cream of tartar dissolved in 1 teaspoon water

Sugar thermometer

Makes 2 cups.

Method
Put the sugar and water into a large saucepan and dissolve the sugar over a low heat. Add the corn syrup or dissolved cream of tartar and bring the mixture to a boil. Boil steadily to the soft ball stage (242°F on a sugar thermometer), then instantly take the pan from the heat, let the bubbles subside and pour the mixture slowly onto a dampened marble slab or into a dampened roasting pan.

Cool the mixture slightly, then work it with a wooden spatula held in each hand until it becomes a firm white mass. Quite suddenly the mixture will become too stiff to work. Take a small piece of fondant at a time, and work it in your hand to make a smooth ball. Pack the balls into a bowl or jar, cover tightly and leave at least 1 hour and preferably for several days to mellow.

To use the fondant: heat it in a bowl set over a pan of hot water; add a little sugar syrup to dilute it, stirring constantly. The dissolved fondant should just coat the back of a spoon and never get hotter than lukewarm or it will lose its gloss.

French Flan Pastry

Sift 1 cup flour onto a board or marble slab and make a large well in the center. Add 4 tablespoons butter, ¼ cup sugar, 2 egg yolks and ½ teaspoon vanilla and work these ingredients with the fingertips of one hand until smooth. Gradually draw in the flour, working with the whole hand, until you have formed a dough. Knead lightly until smooth, then refrigerate for a couple of hours before using.

Makes enough to line 9—12 individual tartlet pans.

MEASURING & MEASUREMENTS

The recipe quantities in the Course are measured in standard level teaspoons, tablespoons and cups and their equivalents are shown below. Any liquid pints and quarts also refer to U.S. standard measures.

When measuring dry ingredients, fill the cup or spoon to overflowing without packing down and level the top with a knife. All the dry ingredients, including flour, should be measured before sifting, although sifting may be called for later in the instructions.

Butter and margarine usually come in measured sticks (1 stick equals $\frac{1}{2}$ cup) and other bulk fats can be measured by displacement. For $\frac{1}{3}$ cup fat, fill the measuring cup $\frac{2}{3}$ full of water. Add fat until the water reaches the 1 cup mark. Drain the cup of water and the fat remaining equals $\frac{1}{3}$ cup.

For liquids, fill the measure to the brim, or to the calibration line.

Often quantities of seasonings cannot be stated exactly, for ingredients vary in the amount they require. The instructions 'add to taste' are literal, for it is impossible to achieve just the right balance of flavors in many dishes without tasting them.

Liquid measure	**Volume equivalent**
3 teaspoons	1 tablespoon
2 tablespoons	1 fluid oz
4 tablespoons	$\frac{1}{4}$ cup
16 tablespoons	1 cup or 8 fluid oz
2 cups	1 pint
2 pints	1 quart
4 quarts	1 gallon

OVEN TEMPERATURES

Fahrenheit	Level of heat
550°	Broil
450°	Very hot
400°	Hot
375°	Moderately hot
350°	Moderate
325°	Moderately low
300°	Low
200°	Very low

OVEN TEMPERATURES AND SHELF POSITIONS

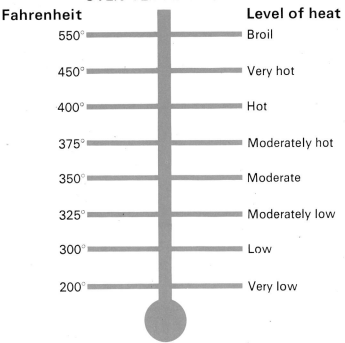

Throughout the Cooking Course, oven temperatures are stated in degrees Fahrenheit and in generally agreed levels of heat such as 'high' and 'moderate'. The equivalents are shown on the table above.

However, exact temperature varies in different parts of an oven and the thermostat reading refers to the heat in the middle. As the oven temperature at top and bottom can vary as much as 25°F from this setting, the positioning of shelves is very important. In general, heat rises, so the hottest part of the oven is at the top, but consult the manufacturer's handbook about your individual model.

Pans and dishes of food should be placed parallel with burners or elements to avoid scorched edges.

When baking cakes, there must be room for the heat to circulate in the oven around baking sheets and cake pans; otherwise the underside of the cakes will burn. If baking more than one cake in an oven that has back burners or elements, arrange the cakes side by side. If the oven has side burners, arrange cakes back and front.

Oven thermostats are often inaccurate and are unreliable at extremely high or low temperatures. If you do a great deal of baking or question the accuracy of your oven, use a separate oven thermometer as a check on the thermostat.

INDEX

(Volume 20)

Index

D

E

F

G

H

I

JK

L

M

NO

P

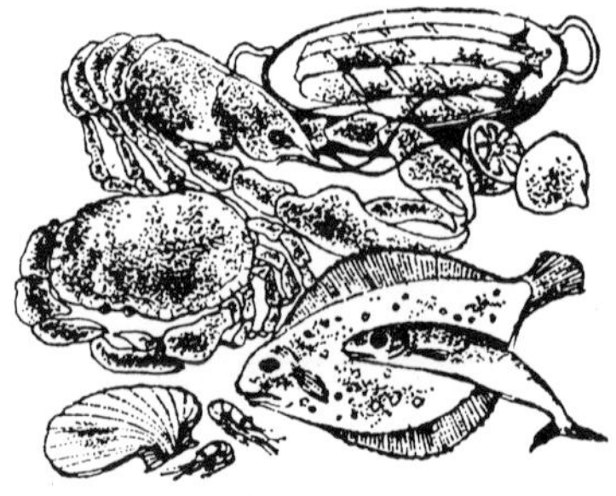

QR

S

T

V

W

YZ

NOTES